THE NEW MANAGER'S
SURVIVAL MANUAL

The New Manager's Survival Manual

All the Skills You Need for Success

CLAY CARR

WILEY

John Wiley & Sons

New York • Chichester • Brisbane • Toronto • Singapore

Library of Congress Cataloging in Publication Data:

Carr, Clay, 1934–
    The new manager's survival manual : all the skills you need for
success / by Clay Carr.
        p.   cm.
    Bibliography: p.
    ISBN 0-471-61375-4.   ISBN 0-471-61696-6 (pbk.)
    1. Supervision of employees.   I. Title.
HF5549.12.C37 1988
658.3'02—dc19   88-10143
                                                                    CIP

Printed in the United States of America
10 9 8 7 6 5 4 3 2 1

To Gayle:
Thanks, Honey

Foreword

If anyone deserves, or needs, a survival manual it is the new manager. Organizations today must face many problematic issues: poor product quality, poor motivation, low morale, conflict and distrust among groups and various levels of the organization, change, time, and finding managers willing to be mentors.

The challenge is overwhelming. Most efforts to assist the new manager lack focus and are so complex as to render them useless. *The New Manager's Survival Manual* is a first-step, straightforward approach—must reading for folks beginning the journey of maximizing the performance of self and others.

PAUL HERSEY
Chairman of the Board
Leadership Studies, Inc.
Author, *The Situational Leader*

Preface

What Is the New Manager's Survival Manual?

You're a new manager. Or you're about to become one. Or you want to become one, so you plan to be prepared when the opportunity comes.

The New Manager's Survival Manual is written for you. It's the basic guide you need to understand first-level management and be effective at it.[1]

This book will

1. Outline the functions of the primary management job: supervising,
2. Explain what you have to do to be a successful first-level manager,
3. Define the basic skills you need and help you begin to develop them,
4. Aid you in setting the right priorities,
5. Start you down the road to successful management—that happy situation where your employees produce, your boss is happy with you, and you are promotable.

---

[1]You may not be familiar with the term "first-level manager." This is the position that's often called "first-level supervisor," or just "supervisor." As Chapter 1 will explain, a "supervisor" is first of all a manager—so we're going to call him or her a manager.

No single book can tell you everything you need to know or even a tenth of what you need to know. In fact, a dozen books won't tell you that.

This book, though, will get you launched in the right direction, learning the right skills. Because it offers you practical tips for each aspect of the job, you'll be prepared to deal with almost anything you encounter.

Reading this book will also be good preparation for your organization's supervisory and/or managerial development program. After you read it, you'll be able to absorb more quickly the formal training you receive. And because this book doesn't teach one particular *way* to manage, it will work with whatever managerial style your organization has.

There's one other point, and it's a sort of pun. "New manager" means someone who has just become a manager—and that's who this book is about. "New manager" can also mean a manager who performs his or her job in an innovative or nontraditional way. This book is about that kind of new manager too.

From one point of view, the type of managing this book advocates isn't new at all; good managers have been doing it this way for years. But traditional books on managing often overlooked this, particularly forgetting to stress that the way a manager gets his or her job done is to develop successful workers and a successful workgroup.

For a variety of reasons, we see the importance of this kind of managing more clearly now. This is a book for new managers who want to be New Managers.

If you're a woman manager (or would-be manager), this final word is addressed to you: Wrestle as I may with it, proper English is irreparably sexist. After a number of attempts, I finally gave in and have used "he" and "him" instead of their more awkward substitutes. I ask you to read through the words to their underlying intent—they simply mean "human being."

CLAY CARR

Westerville, Ohio
September 1988

Acknowledgments

Any book is the product of chains of influence that had their beginnings years ago and wind their way into the present—like multiple strands of DNA. It's impossible to identify the dozens of books and hundreds of people whose imprints are on these pages. But a few are clear enough to note:

Carolyn Sant and Terry Buttars of the Defense Depot in Ogden, Utah. They read the book in outline and raised dozens of helpful questions.

Mary Fletcher and Russ Bronstein of my staff. They read several of the chapters in draft and gave me useful feedback.

Jerry Smith, my deputy for three years. Discussions with him helped shape a number of my ideas.

My bosses, Anthony Hudson—Staff Director of Civilian Personnel for the Defense Logistics Agency (DLA)—and Roberta Peters—the Deputy Staff Director. They put me into a job that challenges me, and they support me in my struggles to perform it.

My editor, John Mahaney, who shaped this book in a number of helpful ways.

Most of all, the staff of the DLA Civilian Personnel Service Support Office. These bright, motivated people keep me on my mental toes and make a book like this possible.

To all of you, my gratitude! Many of the ideas in this book that really sing are yours. Those that sing off-key, I take full responsibility for.

C.C.

Contents

Prologue

"Well, how's the branch's newest supervisor today?" Tim smiled at Louise as he slipped into the chair across from her.

Louise frowned. "Well, in answer to your question, Tim, I'm feeling very frustrated. Aaron called in sick again this morning, Maria and Roger aren't speaking to each other, and we just got four new jobs dumped on us that everybody wants yesterday. Sometimes I don't think I was cut out to be in management."

"I know what you mean," Tim said. "I spent the last hour arguing with Reggie about his performance appraisal. I just can't get him to accept that he does average work. One more hassle like that, and I'm going to give every one of them an 'Above Average' rating and let it go at that—like some people I know have been doing for years." He looked knowingly at Barry, the most experienced of the four managers at the table.

"You're learning." Barry smiled. "The next thing you need to do is take the personnel policies book and hide it. I have an agreement with my people—I don't hassle them, they don't hassle me. I haven't had a grievance or an EEO complaint in so long I don't remember what the forms look like."

"Yeah, I know," Jennie gestured emphatically at Barry with her fork. "You let your people get away with murder while the rest of us get a bad name for trying to do what we're supposed to do. I was here until eight o'clock last night reworking the Emerald Hill project—and I'll probably be here just as late tonight redoing something else that one of my people will screw up today."

Tim nodded. "The people personnel sends you these days won't do anything on their own. If I didn't stand there and tell them what to do, they wouldn't get anything done all day. Sometimes I think I ought to have them call me 'Sarge.'"

Louise frowned and rested her head on her hands. "You're sure not helping any! If that's all management is, I'm sorry I took the job. Isn't there some other way to be a first-level manager and still get the job done? . . ."

THE NEW MANAGER'S
SURVIVAL MANUAL

SUCCESSFUL FIRST-LEVEL MANAGEMENT
(The Skills Maximization Model)

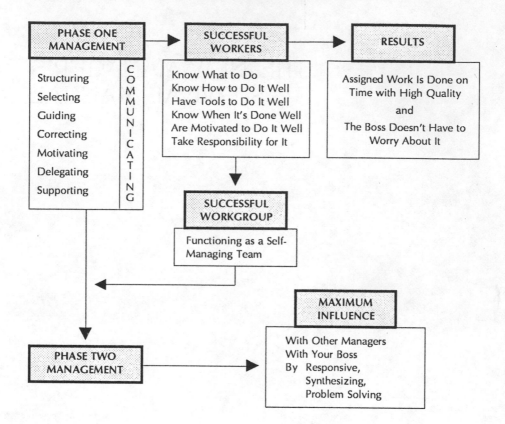

CHAPTER 1

Successful Management: What, How, and the Payoff

A SUCCESSFUL MANAGER
Gets Results
By Developing Successful Workers
and
By Building Influence in the Organization

In this chapter, you'll find useful information about:

The *what* of a manager's job (the two essential functions of a manager).

How a successful manager accomplishes these functions (Phase One and Phase Two Management).

The *payoff* for successful management.

A successful manager sees that the work assigned to his workgroup gets done. Here's how he does it.

Does the title make it sound as though this chapter is going to be complicated and involved? It's not. Everything in it can be summarized in a few short sentences:

If you're a manager, the *what* of your job is to

1. See that your workgroup gets its assigned work done on time, in sufficient quantity, and with high quality; and
2. Do this in such a way that your boss is kept out of trouble and spends a minimum amount of time concerned with your workgroup.

The *how* of your job is accomplished in two phases:

In *Phase One Management*, you develop successful workers.

> **More than anything else you can do, developing successful workers is the key to being successful as a manager.**

Then, when you're successful in Phase One, you have time for *Phase Two*. In this phase, you

1. Develop influence with other managers and significant people, and
2. Have the time and skills to perform special projects for your boss.

When both Phase One and Phase Two are done successfully, this is the *payoff*:

1. You have a skillful and confident workgroup,
2. You're a successful member of your boss's workgroup,
3. You're extremely useful to your organization, and
4. You're promotable.

> **In other words, the best way to get the workgroup's work done is also the way that benefits your workgroup, your boss, your organization, and yourself the most!**

Sound too good to be true? It isn't. Read on and see.

MANAGING IS MANAGING

If you've read carefully to this point, you may have noticed that what a manager does sounds suspiciously like what a "supervisor" does. Congratulations! You win the door prize.

Supervision is management, and all management requires supervision. When you become a supervisor, you become a manager. You cross an invisible, critical line. This is the line:

> When you're a worker, whether a janitor or an attorney, you're responsible only for what *you* produce. When you become a manager, you become responsible for the completion of work that only *others* can accomplish.

From now on, if you are successful, it will be because you are able to get others—your workgroup—to accomplish their assigned work. Your workgroup may be six shipment clerks or the vice-presidents of an international bank. It makes no difference; your first function as a manager is to see that the work assigned to your group is done, done right, and done on time.

If you're a new manager, it means that you've probably moved into a position called "first-level supervisor." That's a common title for the job, but don't let it hide the fact that you're really a manager now. For the rest of the book, this position will be referred to as "first-level manager"—to make it clear that you've crossed the line into management.[1]

SUCCESSFUL MANAGING: PHASE ONE

As said before, a first-level manager's basic function is to see to the completion of things that only others can accomplish. Just what does

---

[1] I asked a friend of mine who's a first-level manager to read the outline of this book. When he came to this point, he wrote in the margin: "Becoming a supervisor should not be considered the first level of management, but should be con'idered as the backbone of the management team." He's right, but you can be both.

that mean? Let's see if we can flesh it out a bit by looking at one manager who's basically succeeding and one who's not doing as well.

George has been a first-level manager in the bindery of a printing plant for four years now. He's one of the hardest workers in the plant, always coming in early and staying late. Because he can't get workers with the skills he wants, he often does the more complicated work himself. Even when he doesn't have to do the whole job, he frequently has to step in and perform a difficult step for a worker. George makes it a point, though, to explain to the worker that he's not expected to be able to do the work— so he won't feel badly about George having to do it.

George believes he should get to know each worker and often stops to chat with them. He tries to find out what's important to them in their personal lives and asks about such. He avoids getting too chummy with them, though, since he often has to reprimand them for failing to do their work properly. In fact, he often complains to his wife about the time he has to spend chewing workers out and doing their work over.

Because of the importance of George's function and because his workforce isn't as good as he would like, George reports to his boss each morning on what the group accomplished the day before. George's boss will often come by once or twice a day, just to see how things are proceeding and to see if George needs help.

Susan has been the other first-level manager in the bindery for about the same length of time, but she has a very different style of managing. She's generally a quiet person who doesn't make small talk with her workers and insists that they call her "Mrs. Evers." She will occasionally pitch in to help her workgroup if they get behind schedule, but insists that otherwise, they do even the hardest work themselves. George thinks she's lazy because she almost never puts in extra time. And she makes a worker do a task over and over until it's done correctly, rather than going ahead and doing it herself.

Instead of spending time checking her people's work to see that it's done right, Susan often leaves her work area entirely and goes to chew the fat with other managers. George gets angry that she can get away with this, and wonders how she managed to get workers so much more reliable than his. It also makes him angry that her group so often gets preferential treatment from other departments.

On the other hand, Susan's boss doesn't spend much time with Susan or her people; most of the time, Susan has to go see her boss. Yet, Susan's boss often picks her to do special projects. George thinks it's unfair that Susan gets rewarded even though she doesn't spend enough time managing her people.

Neither manager is perfect, but have you picked the better one? It's Susan, of course. Were you surprised? The fact of the matter is that she is doing a much better job than George of performing a manager's two basic functions (the *what* of the job):

1. Susan sees that her workgroup gets its assigned work done on time, in sufficient quantity, and with acceptable quality. You or George might not agree with her methods, but they're working.
2. She does this in a way that keeps her boss out of trouble and allows him to spend the least possible time dealing with problems caused by her unit. That's why her boss comes by so seldom; he doesn't *need* to keep close tabs on her.

To understand George and Susan better, look critically at some of the things they do:

George puts in lots of time; he comes to work early and stays late. He has to put in these extra hours because he's doing so much of the work himself. George isn't getting work done *through* others—he's getting work done *instead* of them. His method takes time away from other things he should be doing. Even worse, it keeps each of his workers from learning the full job and taking responsibility for it. (He reinforces this when he points out to workers that they're not expected to be able to do the work.)

Susan communicates something very different to her people. She'll occasionally pitch in to help them, but she doesn't monopolize the hard (and often, most challenging) work. Instead, she insists that each worker do *all* of an assigned job, even the most difficult parts. When a worker makes a mistake, she has *him* do it over; that way, the worker learns how to do it right. Then Susan doesn't have to put in extra hours doing the work herself.

The fact that George wants to get to know each worker is one of his strong points, just as Susan's lack of contact with her group may handicap her. But making friends with their workers isn't an essential part of George and Susan's jobs; it almost never makes or breaks a supervisor.

George also spends lots of time reprimanding his workers for not doing their jobs properly. As you'll see later in this book, the need to repeatedly guide a worker is a sign of a problem. It's not a normal part of management.

You can tell George isn't succeeding because his boss is spending so much time with him and his workgroup. Unless they happen to be bored or like their company, bosses don't spend a lot of time with their successful subordinate managers. They also don't like to spend time following up on work that's the responsibility of the subordinate manager. And they almost never "help" successful managers.

HOW A SUCCESSFUL MANAGER DOES IT

The next chapter describes a successful worker, and the chapters after that explain what a manager has to do to develop successful workers. If you look at the brief description of Susan's workgroup, though, you can catch a glimpse of what successful workers are like.

First of all, they're able to do even the most difficult work themselves. Second, they're reliable; they do the work without anyone looking over their shoulders. That's a lot right there—but the next chapter will show that it's just part of the total picture.

The important point to remember for now is that the way to get your workgroup's work done is to develop your workers into *successful* workers—and your workgroup into a successful workgroup. You don't do the work yourself; you don't force them to do it by over-managing them; and you don't just let them do it however they please. You start with the best people you can hire, and you develop them into successful workers.

Many books concentrate on the *activities* of a manager—what you do everyday. This one does, too. It describes structuring, selecting, guiding, correcting, motivating, delegating, and supporting—all of the things you have to do to develop successful workers. Remember, though, it's the *results* that count:

People in the organization care very much about the results of your Phase One Management—about getting your *function* done successfully. Few people, if any, care about the activities you do to develop successful workers. In other words, you are free to spend as little time as possible on Phase One Management, as long as you produce the right results.

SUCCESSFUL MANAGING: PHASE TWO

Being good at Phase One Management isn't enough. Look at Susan again. Because her workgroup is successful, she has time to spend doing things outside her workgroup. She can build her influence with other supervisors and other people on which she has to rely. (That's why she gets "preferential treatment.") She also has time to do special projects for her boss. Because of this, her boss and other people that matter think she's promotable.

Actually, this is a separate level of management—Phase Two Management. This is all of the things a manager does to develop influence with other managers and with his boss. It's the time Susan spends working with her peers and doing special projects for her boss.

Your first reaction may be that this is self-serving, something done just to promote your own career. It does promote your career, but that's not the only reason you do it. In fact, it's not even the main reason.

Chapters 14 and 15 talk more about Phase Two Management. All that needs to be said about it here is this:

1. All workgroups depend on other groups to be successful. For instance, isn't it much easier to do a job if the people who want it done will work with you—instead of just criticizing when something's done wrong? Isn't it much easier if the supplies you need arrive on time? Good relations with other workgroups can accomplish this.

2. What you can do to develop successful workers depends greatly on what your boss thinks of you. If he sees you as barely competent, you'll never be given the freedom to help your workgroup become successful. If he thinks both you and your workers are competent and dedicated, you'll have room to succeed.

3. How much influence a manager has over his workgroup depends on how much influence the workgroup thinks he has on other managers and on his boss. If the workers think their manager has "clout," they'll do what he wants. If they don't, they probably won't.

ONE MORE TIME . . .

The functions of a manager (the *what*), the means a successful manager uses to become successful (the *how*), and the *payoff* from them hold true for all management jobs. It doesn't matter whether the workers are cashiers or fashion designers, supply clerks or nuclear engineers, computer programmers or department heads.

Whatever kind of organization a manager is in, the two basic functions of management are the same:

1. Develop a workgroup that gets its work done, and
2. Do it in a way that requires your boss to spend a minimum amount of time worrying about it.

The means are the same:

1. Develop successful workers (Phase One Management), and
2. Develop and use influence with other managers and with your boss (Phase Two Management).

And the payoff is still the same:

1. You have a skillful and confident workgroup,
2. You're a successful member of your boss's workgroup,
3. You're extremely useful to your organization, and
4. You're promotable.

THE SKILLS MAXIMIZATION MODEL

"Skills maximization model"—sounds impressive, doesn't it? It describes the model of successful management outlined in this book: a way of managing that gives everyone involved the opportunity to develop and use skills to the maximum.

The model was presented in the front of this book. We've looked at the main components of it in this chapter. This is what we have so far:

The next chapter will fill in more of the details by describing successful workers. But before you go on you might want to use the first Stretch-Meter. What's that? Read on.

STRETCHMETERS AND ASAPS

At the end of most—but not all—of the chapters from now on you'll find "StretchMeters." A StretchMeter is a simple device with a simple function: it helps you evaluate whether, and how much, you need to "stretch" to master the skills described in that chapter.

There's nothing mysterious about a StretchMeter. It's a way for you to evaluate yourself quickly on a set of factors that are relevant to part of the first-level manager's job.

It's easy to use a StretchMeter. Each one has a series of statements describing a quality or a skill. Under each description is a range running from NEVER to ALWAYS. For example:

I spend a great deal of time getting all of the details correct.

NEVER   0   1   2   3   4   5   6   7   8   ALWAYS

You use the StretchMeter by circling the number between NEVER and ALWAYS that best describes you. If you NEVER worry about the details, you would circle 0; if you ALWAYS spend a lot of time on them, you would circle 8. Most of the time, you'll probably circle a number somewhere between the two extremes.

The description above was a sample; it doesn't have a "right" answer where managing is concerned. From now on, the descriptions *will* have "right" answers. These answers are the ones represented by the numbers on the right-hand half of the range. Most of the time, if you can circle the 6 or the 7, you have as much of that quality or skill as you need to be a very effective first-level manager.

Each StretchMeter is made up of a series of descriptions, each followed by a scale like the one in the example. You circle one number on the line below each description. When you've finished that Stretch-Meter, draw a line connecting each of your circles. The closer the overall line is to the right-hand side of the scale, the better your overall score is for that cluster of qualities or skills.

What if part or all of the line is closer to the left-hand side? It means that you need to *stretch* on those qualities or skills in order to be really effective. That's where ASAP—"Adopting Stretching Actions Promptly"—comes in.

Each ASAP contains a set of actions that corresponds to the items in the StretchMeter. If you scored yourself low on Item #3 on the Stretch-Meter, use ASAP 3 to help you start developing that quality or skill.

You don't have to do the ASAP actions, of course—they're there simply to help you. Even if you do them, you won't be magically transformed overnight. But you will have taken the first step on an important journey.

Do you see the picture now? As you read this book and complete the StretchMeters, you'll begin to get an idea of your strengths and weaknesses. (If you didn't have strengths, you wouldn't be a first-level manager. If you didn't have weaknesses, you wouldn't be human.) Then you can choose the ASAP actions you want to do to start turning weaknesses into strengths.

One other thought: You might want to have a friend—someone you can trust to be honest with you—complete some of the StretchMeters on you, too. If the two of you come up with very different results (more than two numbers apart, for example), then you may want to ask yourself if you're really being objective. Or you may be right about yourself but don't always communicate what you're really like to others.

The first StretchMeter measures some of the personal qualities that it helps to have if you're going to be a manager. None of them are absolutely necessary; in fact, there are good managers who lack some of them. On the whole, though, you'll do a better job (and do it more easily) if you have or develop most of these qualities.

To help you become used to Adopting Stretching Actions Promptly (ASAP), an ASAP has been included following this first StretchMeter. However, there is a basic difference between this meter and all other ones.

All other StretchMeters ask you to rate yourself on specific, limited skills. If you rate yourself toward the low end, it simply means you don't have that skill fully developed yet. The ASAP for that StretchMeter will get you started toward acquiring the skill.

This StretchMeter measures *qualities*—which are broad, deeply ingrained personal traits or characteristics. They reflect skills; for instance, the ability to approach tense situations objectively is a skill. However, they go much deeper than that, and acquiring them involves *unlearning* old behaviors.

For this reason, the short exercise presented in the first ASAP will barely scratch the surface. If you rate yourself below where you believe you should be in one or more qualities, you may want to look for a book or a course dealing with that specific quality—or perhaps try to learn from someone you respect who has that quality.

Don't give up or take a pessimistic attitude. Each of us can change very basic traits and qualities if determined to do it and willing to spend the effort. You should understand, though, that qualities do not change easily—and be prepared to invest the time and energy needed to make the change.

Enough talk—on to StretchMeter 1.

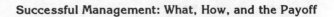

StretchMeter 1: DESIRABLE MANAGEMENT QUALITIES

1. I enjoy being with people.

NEVER   0   1   2   3   4   5   6   7   8   ALWAYS

2. I approach tense situations very objectively.

NEVER   0   1   2   3   4   5   6   7   8   ALWAYS

3. I can deal positively with frustrated people.

NEVER   0   1   2   3   4   5   6   7   8   ALWAYS

4. I enjoy helping other people learn.

NEVER   0   1   2   3   4   5   6   7   8   ALWAYS

5. I'm comfortable letting others take the credit.

NEVER   0   1   2   3   4   5   6   7   8   ALWAYS

6. I can stay calm when someone interrupts me.

NEVER   0   1   2   3   4   5   6   7   8   ALWAYS

7. I can enjoy people who are different from me.

NEVER   0   1   2   3   4   5   6   7   8   ALWAYS

8. I prefer to act on my own, not wait to be told what to do.

NEVER   0   1   2   3   4   5   6   7   8   ALWAYS

9. Others will usually listen to me and do what I ask.

NEVER   0   1   2   3   4   5   6   7   8   ALWAYS

Desirable Management Qualities ASAP

1. One of the best ways to get to know your workers is also a good way to start enjoying being with them—share lunch or a break with them. For the next two weeks, plan to have lunch or a break with each worker in your workgroup at least once. You'll find plenty of reasons for not doing it, but don't let anything stop you. Do it. You may want to keep on doing it long after the two weeks are over.

2–3. A basic reason for reacting emotionally in tense situations or reacting negatively toward frustrated people is that the reaction "grabs" you before you have a chance to think. You need something to remind you not to react before you have time to think:

If you have a desk, find a simple object that doesn't belong there and place it in clear view. That object is now your official *Reaction Alert*. You're going to use it to remind yourself that you aren't going to react negatively. You're going to be calm and positive, no matter what. Every time you look at it, remember that. When someone comes in who's frustrated, use the object to remind yourself not to fall into your habitual negative response, and make a different response instead.[2]

If you don't have an office, or if you're often away from it, there's another method that often works. Carry around a small counter—such as the type that golfers use to record their scores. This is your portable Reaction Alert. Whenever you run into a frustrated individual and react negatively, punch the counter. It's remarkable how this will help you become aware of the problem.[3]

If neither of these sounds good to you, find another way. What you do doesn't matter. What does matter is that you find a reliable way to make yourself aware of your habitual reflex. Once you become

[2]To deal with a similar problem, I use an 8-inch green foam ball. It sits right in the middle of my desk. I've also told my staff why it's there, so that we all know the situation we're trying to avoid. It works! (The idea, by the way, came from working with Merilee Zdenek, president of Right-Brain Resources in Reseda, Calif.)

[3]This idea comes from a book called *Precision Nirvana* by Deane H. Shapiro, Jr. (Englewood Cliffs, N.J.: Prentice-Hall, 1978).

aware of it, you gain the power to *choose* how to respond. Choosing is the name of the game.

4. One reason you may not enjoy helping other people learn is that you don't think of this as an important duty. You may think to yourself, "Oh, alright, I'll help him for a few minutes—then I'll get back to *my* job." If that's the case, you can manage this trait just by deciding that helping others learn *is* part of your job. It is. Helping others learn, or *guiding* them, is one of the seven critical activities of a manager. Don't wait until you read that chapter, though; decide now, *right now*, that helping people learn is important— and do it.

5. Letting other people take the credit can be very difficult for anyone. One reason is that you may be telling yourself that if someone else takes the credit, you can't have it. When you're a manager, that's not true; you get to take credit for everything your workers do. So, within the next week, help at least two of your workers accomplish something (perhaps just get a task done on time or early) and then see that they get credit for it.

6. If you have trouble staying calm when interrupted, use the same technique given in ASAP 2—your Reaction Alert. A word of caution, though: *Don't* use the same reminder for two different purposes at the same time. In fact, you should deal with only one trait at a time, even if you rated yourself low in both. Get the first under control, then attack the second.

7. If you don't enjoy people who are different from you, you may have difficulty in managing them. As you get to know such people, their "differences" often fade away, and you can see them as just plain people. In the short run, you can use a Reaction Alert (see ASAP 2) and record each time you have stereotyped a person with your own negative reaction. That will at least make sure you're aware of your feelings—and that's a beginning.

8. As you'll see as you read this book, most of what a successful manager does is done on his own. In the next two weeks, find at least one small task a day that you can do without waiting for someone to tell you to do it. (The small task may be part of a larger task. For instance, if you want to wait until someone tells you it's

okay to begin a new procedure, you can prepare all of the written copies of the procedure now to be handed out later.)

9. Having others listen to you and follow you is the mark of a leader— and you may not have thought of yourself as a leader before. There's no quick, easy way to become a leader. Unfortunately, becoming a manager doesn't make you one. If you practice Phase One and Phase Two Management conscientiously, though, you will become a leader.

A FINAL WORD

If you read the different ASAP items, you saw how many times a Reaction Alert could be useful. That's helpful learning right there. When you have trouble making a change you want to make, it's often because you make the habitual reaction before you realize it. You become aware of what you're doing *after* you've started to do it. Then it's usually too late to act differently.

The key is finding a way to become aware *before* you act. This is the purpose of a Reaction Alert. You'll find that some kind of Reaction Alert is one of the best aids you can have for effective change.

The two Reaction Alerts described previously actually work slightly differently. The one on your desk is designed to remind you *not* to react. The counter in your pocket probably won't do that. But it will let you tally up the number of times you reacted without thinking—and this will help you become aware of it.

You might find that something else works better for you. Go for it! The idea is to find something that will stop the reaction before it commits you to the behavior you want to change.

CHAPTER 2

The Successful Worker

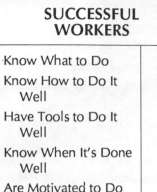

SUCCESSFUL WORKERS
Know What to Do
Know How to Do It Well
Have Tools to Do It Well
Know When It's Done Well
Are Motivated to Do It Well
Take Responsibility for It

In this chapter, you'll find useful information on the characteristics of a successful worker.

The goal of Phase One Management is to develop successful workers. This chapter describes what makes workers successful.

WHAT IS A SUCCESSFUL WORKER?

Elena Radice has been at Wendell Products since she graduated from high school three years ago. She started in the typing pool but moved to accounts payable two years ago. Although she likes accounting work, she's taking courses at night to become a paraprofessional.

In the meantime, she does her job well. She learned it from Harry Tomlin, the section supervisor. Harry worked closely with her for several days when she first started. He explained the system to her and showed her each of the formats that were used. Then he took her on a tour of the rest of the accounting department, to see how the data she input was used in the system as a whole.

The manual for the bookkeeping system worried her at first; it was very big and seemed quite complicated. Harry sat down and went through its basic structure with her. Then he gave her a group of transactions, showed her the chapter that described how to process them, and had her do them. When she had gotten them done correctly, he gave her a different group and showed her a different chapter. Before long, she knew how to do all of the routine transactions and where she could find the rules for the difficult ones.

While the manual was helpful, she soon found that it wasn't enough. Then Harry gave her some desk guides that other workers in the group had made up, and these were a great help. The workgroup had also developed worksheets for the most complicated transactions.

As soon as she was able to do a range of transactions, Harry explained her "responsibility code." At the beginning of the day, she typed her code into the computer. Then the code was added to every transaction she processed. "It lets you know if any of them have been done incorrectly," Harry explained. "If one of the transactions has to be returned because of an error, it comes right back to you to correct. I won't even know about it unless you make too many errors—then I'll get a printout, and I can help you figure out what's causing the mistakes." It wasn't long before Elena started to look at all of the transactions she produced as "hers."

Elena wants to do a good job since she knows she will probably have to work for several years. The rest of the workgroup is conscientious, which helps. And whenever they have a particularly good day—very few errors—Harry posts the summary with "GOOD JOB!" on it in big letters.

Elena is good enough that she doesn't often have to ask others how to do a particular transaction, and she takes pride in seeing how long she can go without having one returned because of an error.

In other words, Elena is a good worker, who:

1. Knows what to do,
2. Knows how to do it well,
3. Has the tools with which to do it,
4. Knows when she has done it well,
5. Is motivated to do it well, and
6. Takes responsibility for it.

KNOWING WHAT TO DO   *also pg 20 -(1-3)*

This sounds pretty obvious, doesn't it? Of course a worker should know what to do. But let's look at what can happen:

Van's boss calls him and tells him that the auditing department needs a report showing all the trips each auditor makes each month. Van identifies all of the fields in the database that he needs and creates a complete report showing each auditor and the trips he made. (Van doesn't know that when the report gets to auditing, a secretary will make a list of the dates that auditors visited each location—which is the only information the auditing department really needs.)

Every morning John gets his priority orders out first. This takes extra time because a lot of the stock for the routine orders is the same as that for the priority orders—which means he has to make two trips to the same area a lot of the time. But John was told that the priority stock needed to be picked first, and because he's conscientious, he tries to have all priority orders done and out the door by 9:00 A.M. (What the person who told him actually meant was that the priority orders must be ready to be picked up by 1:00 P.M.)

Jennie is responsible for drafting replies to congressmen who write letters to headquarters about the district office in which she

works. She spends a great deal of time on each letter, making sure
that she has each word just right. (She doesn't know that when the
public relations office gets her letter, it is rewritten completely using
a specific format.)

These examples illustrate how slippery "doing the right thing" can be.
Jennie, John, and Van are all wasting time because they don't know why
their work is done, or when it needs to be done, or what the people who
need their work do with it.

They're all conscientious workers who want to do a good job. From
their points of view, they *are* doing a good job. In reality, they're less
productive than necessary, only because they haven't been told important particulars about their jobs.

Remember, knowing what to do includes

1. Knowing *when* to do it,
2. Knowing *why* to do it, and
3. Knowing *what* the people you do it for (your customers) do with it.

Workers know what to do only if they receive effective guiding and
correcting. Chapters 6 and 7 of the book cover this.

KNOWING HOW TO DO IT WELL

We all know how important training is. Workers can't do a good job if
they don't know *how* to do it. But, if you want to succeed as a manager,
just seeing that your people are trained isn't enough. You need to see that
all of your workers know how to do their jobs *well*.

Here's a quick look at a workgroup where everyone knows how to do
his job:

Ann produces very high quality reports, but it takes her a long
time to do them. Jerry doesn't produce as good a report, but he can
really whip them out. Oscar is a good solid worker, but he has a hard
time getting reports out by their deadlines. Marie is the star; she
produces good reports, does them quickly, and always meets her
deadlines.

Your first reaction may be that, like all workgroups, this one is made up of individual workers, with individual differences. That's right, and it's an important point. But there's another way to look at it. Ann, Jerry, and Oscar know how to do their jobs. Marie knows how to do her job *well.*

Ann and Marie have a good sense of what makes a high quality report; they could probably teach this to the others. Jerry and Marie could probably show Ann and Oscar how to organize and execute their work efficiently and how to meet their deadlines. Then all four workers would know how to do the job well.

It's important that workers know how to do their jobs well, which includes doing quality work that's right the first time. This book will give a lot of attention to this, particularly in Chapters 6 and 7.

HAVING THE TOOLS TO DO IT WELL

This is something else that sounds very obvious. That doesn't mean it always happens:

Sheri spends a lot of time sitting and waiting for her personal computer to compute. She has a really powerful machine, but the spreadsheet she uses is extremely slow. Since she does a lot of "what if" projections, she has to recalculate constantly. It sometimes takes a minute to do a recalculation, and she has to do dozens of them. She's asked for a faster spreadsheet program, but it doesn't look like she'll get one. It's organization policy to buy all software from the company that handles this spreadsheet in order to get a discount.

Ed deals with computers in a different way—he helps manufacture them. Specifically, he attaches the last part to a hard disk drive and puts the drive on a conveyor belt. The procedures for his job say that he should put the drive on a cushioned pad before placing it on the belt. When there are pads there, Ed uses them. Otherwise, he just puts the drive on the belt. Since the pads aren't always there, he figures they can't be all that important. (He doesn't know that a drive which doesn't have a pad is three times as likely to fall off the belt and be damaged.)

As you can see, there are two parts to this point:

1. Having the *right* tools for the job,
2. Having them reliably at hand.

In the real world, one or both often get overlooked. Ed's company knew that a lot of its disk drives were being rejected, but it took several weeks to find out why. Sheri's organization still doesn't know how much of her time is wasted by using the wrong tool.

Chapter 10 deals with the importance of providing a constant supply of the right tools.

TELLING WHEN IT'S DONE WELL

"Mr. Augustine, how do I tell if I'm doing a good job?"
"No problem, Angelina. Around here, if no one is yelling at you, you're doing okay."

Does that sound like your experience? Have you worked in an organization whose basic performance information system was "no news is good news" (NNGN)? What was your reaction to it?

If Angelina is an experienced worker who is performing well—producing sufficient high-quality work on time—the NNGN feedback system will work. There really isn't much her manager needs to tell her. If her performance is below or above this level, though, she needs to know it—no matter how experienced she is.

If Angelina is a new worker, however, and not sure yet just what doing the job well *is*, NNGN is a lousy system. In this circumstance, she needs to know when she's meeting expectations just as much as she needs to know when she's performing above or below standard.

Some very sharp people have been known to say that the biggest single cause of low performance—even of experienced workers—is lack of this feedback. There's another problem: any worker who can't tell how well he or she is doing is at the mercy of the supervisor's opinion. Even if the supervisor is right, most workers really resent being in that position. That's why formal performance ratings are usually (1) a hassle and (2) inflated.

When a worker can tell how good a job he's doing, it increases that worker's control over his own work. For most workers, this leads to performance improvement—without anything else needing to be done. There are some very practical suggestions on how to create this situation later in this book, especially in Chapter 7.

MOTIVATED TO DO IT WELL

Edgar Miller was kicking off his quarterly management refresher course: "All right, I want each of you to list the three most serious problems you have on your job."

There was a flurry of paper shuffling and pencil scratching.

"Okay," he said. "Now, all of you who wrote down 'Motivating Employees' raise your hands."

All of the hands went up.

A manager has an impossible job if his workers don't care—and every smart manager knows this. There simply isn't enough time in the day to do everything else *and* try constantly to motivate workers, too.

"I just can't seem to motivate my workers," said the man in the pink shirt, who was sitting in the first row.

"Exactly," Edgar said.

A murmur went through the class. Edgar waited a moment, then said, "You can't motivate your workers. Either they motivate themselves, or they won't be motivated. Workers will always do what they think pays off for them."

"Then why bother?" the man asked.

"That's simple. Your job is to arrange things for your workgroup so that what pays off for them is doing the kind of job you want done."

This point is worth repeating and emphasizing:

People do what they believe pays off for them. If you want them to do their job well for you, make sure that doing it well pays off— and doing it poorly doesn't.

Here's a quick example of what this means:

Jonathan has moved into the city from a farm and taken a job with the state compensation office. He finds after only two months that he can easily process twice the average number of claims. As soon as he tries though, the other workers accuse him of "showing off." He tries a little longer, but it doesn't seem to matter to his boss. Now he processes just a little more than the average number and is looking for another job.

Jonathan has run into a double whammy:

1. He's being punished for doing well (his fellow workers criticize him for it), and
2. He and everyone else are rewarded for doing so-so work (because there's no reward for doing better).

Chapter 8 will give you ideas on how to avoid these whammies.

TAKING RESPONSIBILITY FOR IT

"Hey, Charlie, c'mon. We're waiting for you."
"Just a minute, Arnie. I don't have this solder joint right yet."
"Ah, let it go. One of the inspectors will catch it and send it back."
"Not on your life. In the first place, if an inspector catches it, he'll know it's mine. In the second place, it is mine—and I'm going to get the damned thing right."

Charlie understands what it takes to be a successful worker. If a worker knows what to do and how to do it, uses his tools effectively, knows when he's done a job well, and is motivated, that worker is still not successful until he takes responsibility for his work. Charlie takes pride in his work and takes responsibility for it, too.

When a worker takes responsibility for his work, it is done without intervention from you—unless he runs into something he doesn't understand. Otherwise, his work is done in the right quantity, in conformance with quality standards, and on time.

THE PAYOFF

One more time—a successful worker:

1. Knows what to do (and when to do it, why it is to be done, and what customers need from it),
2. Knows how to do it well,
3. Has the tools with which to do it,
4. Knows when he has done it well,
5. Is motivated to do it well, and
6. Takes responsibility for it.

When you have a workgroup made up of successful workers, the payoff for you is tremendous. As you go through this book, you'll see just how tremendous it is. Just as important, there's a tremendous payoff for the workers:

1. Because they're successful, they feel good about themselves, their workgroup, and their work.
2. Because they feel good about their work and each other, they can work closely together—as a team. This makes each individual even more successful, which makes the team stronger, which makes each individual more successful. . . .
3. Because they're successful—individually and together—they manage themselves. This gets them largely out of the boss–subordinate relationship that fewer and fewer workers *and* managers are comfortable with these days.[1]

Convinced? In the next chapter, you'll start learning the skills required to produce successful workers and a successful workgroup.

---

[1]This isn't a minor matter. Research data gathered by the McFletcher Corporation of Scottsdale, Ariz., indicate that:

1. One-third of workers entering the work force don't want to be supervised, and
2. Three-fourths of current first-level managers would like to spend less time supervising.

A BRIEF POSTSCRIPT

The rest of this book is about the specific activities it takes for a manager to be successful. Don't forget, though, that a manager is a worker, too. You're part of your boss's workgroup. When you become a successful supervisor, by practicing successful Phase One and Phase Two Management, you will

1. Know what to do,
2. Know how to do it well,
3. Know what tools you need to do it well,
4. Know when you have done it well,
5. Be motivated to do it well, and
6. Take responsibility for it.

MORE OF THE SKILLS MAXIMIZATION MODEL

In the last chapter, several key components of the skills maximization model were described. This chapter added the characteristics of successful workers. Here are the parts of the model that have been described in this book so far:

CHAPTER 3

Developing Successful Workers

PHASE ONE MANAGEMENT	
Structuring	C
Selecting	O
Guiding	M
Correcting	M
Motivating	U
Delegating	N
Supporting	I
	C
	A
	T
	I
	N
	G

In this chapter, you'll find overall information on the Phase One activities required to develop successful workers:

Structuring,

Selecting,

Guiding,

Correcting,

Motivating,

Delegating, and then

Supporting them.

You'll also find that good communication skills are essential for all of these activities.

This chapter presents a brief overview of the seven activities and the communication skills required to be a successful first-level manager.

A BRIEF CONVERSATION

"Good morning, Mr. Sugeno."

"Good morning, Shirley. Welcome to your first day as a first-level manager."

"Thanks. I think I'm ready for it."

"I'm sure you are. Have you had a chance to look at that survival manual for new managers that I gave you last week?"

"I won't pretend I've read all of it, but I have looked at the first of it."

"Good—that's really what I'm concerned about. Since you're starting as a new first-level manager, I'd like you to be familiar at least with the basic activities of Phase One Management."

"Whew! At least I got that far."

"Would you tell me what these activities are? Don't worry about quoting the book; just put them in your own words."

"Let me see. There are seven of them, right?"

Mr. Sugeno nodded.

"I remember the first one—it's *structuring*. Structuring means planning and organizing the work flow and setting priorities so there are no delays due to confusion within the workgroup. Planning means anticipating workload and being ready for it; organizing means deciding who's going to do what; setting priorities means deciding which tasks are the most important. If you do these right, the workgroup knows *what* they have to do, and *how* it needs to be done, and *when*."

"Excellent," Mr. Sugeno said. "Which reminds me that I have some details about next month's workload that I need to discuss with you and the other section chiefs. We'll do that later; right now, tell me about activity 2."

"The second activity is *selecting*, and I already know how important that is. I can see how quickly I'll get into trouble if I don't find workers who are able and willing to do the work, or if my workers aren't adaptable to the work and the workgroup. I'm lucky; Mrs. Winston was good at this, and she left me a good workgroup."

Mr. Sugeno smiled. "I'm counting on you to prove I'm good at it, too. Anyway, on to activity 3."

"The third one is . . . oh yes, the third one is *guiding*. After you've got workers selected, you have to see that they know what to do and how to do it. I can see from my own experience that an important part of knowing what to do is knowing *when* to do it, *why* it's done, and *who* you're doing it for. You know, when I first started here, it took me a year and a half to find out why I was doing the monthly summary. When I found out, I was amazed at how many different ways it's used."

Mr. Sugeno started to say something, but Shirley kept going: "The next activity is *correcting*, and I remember it because it fits right in with guiding. It's an important idea for me, because I've always thought of correcting as criticizing—and I don't like to criticize people. Now I understand that correcting is really giving useful feedback to people, and I feel better about it. I just hope I can get my workgroup feeling that good about it."

"I think you can. I'd suggest that you start by getting to know your people and letting them know what you expect. After you've been in the job a few weeks, I'm sure I'll hear what their first reactions are, and I'll be glad to share them with you. Anyway, we're up to activity 5, aren't we?"

"Yes, and I suppose that it's the one that sounds the hardest to me. *Motivating* other people just sounds difficult. It did help me some when I read that my job isn't really to motivate them but to create an environment, a job structure, and a reward system that motivates them. That sounds like something I can do, even if it does take me awhile."

"You can, and it probably will. Keep in mind that we pay a bonus to any workgroup that beats its monthly quota by 20 percent—and the supervisor gets part of the bonus. For now, though, tell me about activity 6."

"That's *delegating*, and it's going to be something brand new for me. Effective delegating means that I give each worker the most complete delegation he can handle at that moment. The goal is for me to develop my workgroup to the point where the workers can do their jobs without me looking over their shoulders. Each delegation should stretch them a little, but I need to be realistic and not delegate more than they can handle. I expect to find this quite challenging."

"It is. Why don't you keep some notes on what you've delegated to each of your people, and let's get together Friday at nine o'clock to go over it. I hope you understand that this is just temporary. It won't be long before I'll leave those decisions completely up to you. Now, tell me about activity 7."

"That's *supporting* my people. It means letting them do their jobs and backing them up when they do—even if they do their work differently than I would have done. I can remember a couple of times when I made decisions and my boss didn't back me up—and it was painful for me. I'm certainly going to try to give my workers the training and the tools they need, and then stay out of their way and let them perform. I hope I can count on you to come talk to me if you think one of my people has goofed up. After all, I'm the one who'll delegate the responsibilities to them, so I'm the one you should chew on."

"I see you understand a lot about supporting your people already. You let me know if any of the other section chiefs give you a hard time, and I'll talk to them. I wouldn't have picked you for this job if I didn't think I could rely on you to give me your best. We've gone over the seven activities, but isn't there something we've left out?"

"Yes, but it isn't really an activity. It's *communication*. Good communication skills are what make it possible for a manager to do the seven activities effectively. This part of the manual really surprised me. I thought it would start off by talking about persuasion skills, but they came last. It said that it is more important for a manager to be open and honest; to be able to speak and write clearly; to listen responsively; and to give and seek feedback. If I can do all that, it won't take much more for me to be very effective at persuasion."

"I think you will be, too. Frankly, I was a little concerned about the short time you've been with us when I selected you for the job. As I listen to you, though, I hear some real enthusiasm and forcefulness in your approach. I'm convinced that you'll fit in well with our management style here. Let's see if you really remember what you've told me. Quickly, now, what are the seven activities?"

"Structuring, selecting, guiding, correcting, motivating, delegating, and supporting. And before you ask, the basis for doing all this effectively is good communication. How's that?"

"Excellent. Well, you'd better get in there and get to work."

"Yes, I'd better. Oh, here's your book back."

"From what you said, I thought you liked it."

"I do—so I bought my own copy."

"I'm glad I loaned it to you. Before you go, though, tell me where I can read about the seven activities and good communication skills."

"Oh, that's easy. The next eight chapters tell all about them."

CHAPTER 4

Structuring

PHASE ONE MANAGEMENT	
Structuring	C
Selecting	O
Guiding	M
Correcting	M
Motivating	U
Delegating	N
Supporting	I
	C
	A
	T
	I
	N
	G

In this chapter, you'll find useful information on:

> What effective structuring is and why it's important for success as a manager.
>
> How to plan work.
>
> How to organize work.
>
> How to set priorities.
>
> How to handle required programs.

Structuring will not directly help you develop successful workers. However, when you effectively structure the work of your workgroup, everyone is able to concentrate on doing his job successfully.

WHAT IS EFFECTIVE STRUCTURING?

Perhaps Eula Jefferson learned the importance of getting organized while she was a secretary for five years. Or perhaps it was while she held down a job, raised two boys, and went to night school to finish her degree. Whenever it was, she learned it well.

The managers who work with her keep asking what her secret is. She laughs. "There isn't any secret," she says. "It's just getting things arranged so my people and I aren't the bottleneck."

She certainly does that. As soon as she finds out that a project is coming their way, she calls a "skull session" with her workgroup. (She picked up that term from her football-playing sons.) Together she and the group make their best estimate of the time the project will take. She looks at the schedules for their other projects; if it looks like there will be a time conflict, she makes notes to discuss the problem with her boss and get it resolved.

When she sees that the workgroup's scheduling will permit them to take on the new project, they start to work out who will do it. Sometimes one worker can do the job alone; other times, it takes several working together. They agree on the critical milestones for the project. If it's going to be done by a group of workers, Eula makes sure that every person in the group knows who will do what.

When the project arrives, the workgroup is prepared for it. They know what to do and who will do it. As Eula likes to say, "If you've done your planning and organizing, and set your priorities, the execution's a snap." (She picked that phrase up from her sons, too.)

WHY IS EFFECTIVE STRUCTURING IMPORTANT?

Eula's boss can answer that one for you:

"The gentleman who headed the section before Eula took over was a whiz in the field, but he just wasn't any good at structuring his workgroup. When a new project hit the group, he and the workers would run around in circles trying to figure who was going to do what. When he tried to assign it to various people, they'd all tell him that they were already working on another hot project that had to get done. Once he finally got the new work assigned, not only would it end up being behind schedule, but it would make another two or three projects late along with it.

"Everybody in the section really liked him, but he drove them nuts every time a new project came along. It's the difference between night and day since he got a transfer and Eula took over the job. Now I can count on getting their work on schedule, and they probably produce 20 percent more than they did before Eula stepped in. There hasn't been much change in personnel. It's just that they all know what they're doing and what they're going to do."

HOW DO I STRUCTURE EFFECTIVELY?

There are three aspects of structuring: *planning, organizing*, and *setting priorities*. None of them is any more important than any other, but planning is the first step.

Planning

Arnold Svensen has spent a lot of time learning about planning. Now he's an expert at it. Sometimes he knows when a heavy workload is going to hit his group, and sometimes he doesn't. He's learned how to be prepared either way. Here are some of the things he and his people do:

1. They gather all of the intelligence they can about what's happening "upstream," in the part of the organization where their workload originates. Arnold spends a few hours every week talking with managers involved with work that may come to him. That way, he always has some idea of when new work will arrive—even if he hasn't heard anything officially. He encourages his people to keep *their* eyes and ears open, too. He can't prevent every surprise, but he comes close.

2. Arnold stays abreast of the status of all the work in his group. That

way, when new work comes in he doesn't have to go find out when his people will have time for it. He pays particular care to jobs that are slipping or are ahead of schedule, so they don't catch him by surprise either. Because his people have learned how important planning is, they keep one another up-to-date as well.

3. Arnold insists on being realistic when he plans out a job. He has a reputation for being "hard-nosed," but to him it's just being practical. Things almost never go as well as they could, and he allows room for delays. The managers who gripe at him because he gives realistic dates also know that he will deliver when he says he will. (In fact, he has a sign on his wall that says "Underpromise and Overdeliver"[1] and every so often he lectures his workgroup on it.)

4. Finally, Arnold always makes plans, but he never lets his group or his boss "fall in love" with them. He's seen too many situations where plans were set in concrete. When something happens that disrupts the plans, everybody gets uptight and has to let off a lot of steam before they can get on with the work of making the changes. He stresses to his workgroup that a plan may be what they use for now, but when conditions change, the plan changes too. That way, the group knows where it's going but stays light enough on its feet to change quickly.

EXAMPLE: Effective Planning

Now that Arnold knows for sure when the Western project is coming in, he meets with his three senior workers.

First, he describes the project to them and gives them a chance to ask questions. When this is over, they all know the basic requirements of the project. Arnold has also made a list of several important questions that need to be answered.

Then Arnold has each worker review for the group the status of his most important jobs. Arnold summarizes on the blackboard what each one says. When they finish this step, they all have a good idea about where the new project can be fitted in.

---

[1]Copied, no doubt, from Tom Peters' book, *Thriving on Chaos*. (New York: Alfred A. Knopf, 1987). See "Your Own Management University" at the end of this book.

Arnold then assigns the project to Evelyn. Since adding the new project overloads her, he transfers another project from her to Howard. Then he asks Ben and Marie to work on specific parts of the project with Evelyn.

He leaves the last step to Evelyn, Ben, and Marie—designing the basic plan. He gives them two days to come up with:

1. A description of each important step, and
2. The date when each step will be completed (the "milestones" for the project).

When Evelyn gets back to him with the plan, he approves it as they wrote it, with one exception. They don't expect to have the first action completed until six weeks after the start. Arnold is uncomfortable waiting this long to be sure they're "on track," so he asks them to give him an interim report after three weeks. The basic planning is now complete.

(**WHAT IF** Arnold's workgroup weren't sufficiently advanced to share in the planning to this extent? How might he have done the basic planning— but still involved at least some workers in a way that would help them learn to plan?)

Organizing

"It doesn't do a lot of good to plan if you don't get things organized so you can carry the plan out." That's what Betty Rigelski would tell you. "Organizing means taking your plans and seeing that they go as you expect them to. These are some of the things it takes:

"First of all, you have to have a good plan. If it's unrealistic, too optimistic, or based on bad information, no amount of organizing will save you. At my previous job we'd get our projects in big batches. My manager wanted to make everybody happy, so he'd promise things we couldn't deliver. We'd juggle jobs all over the place and still end up late. If you start with a poor plan, you're going to end with screwed-up organization.

"The second thing is that you have to have the right people doing the right things. If you had the perfect organization, everybody would be great at all the jobs. But in reality, you know that it works better if certain people take certain parts of the job. I think it's because they feel that particular steps are 'their kinds of jobs,' and they put more of themselves into such tasks. (I do try to get the person who is particularly good at something to show the others how to do it well.)

"Of course, you have to be careful here, too, or people will get burned out or stereotyped. I try to make sure that everybody gets a chance at some of the most difficult work and that everybody gets some variety.

"So you start with a good plan, and you give it to the right people. Then you have to make sure that you're on top of things. I don't bug my people with a bunch of formal reports, and I don't keep asking them how things are going. I do make sure they give me a status report as often as necessary. And they know to tell me if they get ahead of or behind schedule. That way, I don't get any surprises. They know that while I trust them to do the work, I still care about it. And when one of the summaries is due, they have to stop for a minute and see just where they are.

"I guess the last thing about organizing is the most important: Everybody concerned with a job needs to know just who's going to do what. It took me a long time to learn what this means.

"When I started out as a first-level manager, I took this idea literally. I thought about every detail and made sure I assigned it to someone. I gradually found out how wasteful this was; some of my people would have nothing to do while others were working their heads off. Worst of all, I'd ask about something, and someone would say, 'That's Charlie's job—ask him.'

"From there I went to the other extreme. I'd get a team together and give it the project. Then I'd tell the members to get it done however they wanted. Sometimes this worked, and I still use it when I have the right team. Many times it didn't work, and important things wouldn't get done because each member of the team thought someone else was doing them.

"I guess I'm somewhere between those two extremes now. I make sure that the team identifies all the major tasks and that it has a system for seeing that each one gets done. Several teams have started making up a checklist of all the tasks on a job. The members meet every so often— depending on the job—to see that someone is handling each task. This way nothing falls through the cracks, and they can trade tasks around to balance out people's workloads."

EXAMPLE: Organizing

Betty was true to her first requirement: as soon as she knew the date of the office move, she developed a realistic plan for it. She had to have the plan first in order to organize effectively.

Because Betty's people are used to working together, she lets them decide who will do the project. She reserves the right to make the final choice, but the appropriate individuals volunteer and she selects them. In fact, one of the people whom she wants to get experience in this kind of work asks to be on the team.*

The next step is to discuss any possible major problems and how they might be handled. This lets Betty tell her group at what point she wants to be notified that a problem is developing. ("If Supply thinks it will have trouble getting us the cartons, let me know right away.") Betty also reminds her workers to let her know about any schedule changes—so she can work them into their overall planning.

Since the team's leader is inexperienced in leading a team, Betty has him give her a list of the major tasks, showing who will do them. The two of them go over the list to make sure that someone has been assigned to each important job. Betty suggests to the leader that he get the team together every two weeks just to make sure that everyone agrees on who's doing what.

Then she turns the project over to the team.

(**WHAT IF** the person whom Betty wanted to get the experience hadn't volunteered? How could Betty have gotten that worker onto the team without forcing him?)

---

*Have you noticed that picking the people for the team has shown up under planning and organizing? For good reason: Most of the time, planning and organizing overlap each other. (This is particularly true when it's done with or by the workers involved.) In a book, we can say, "This is planning," and, "That is organizing." In the real world, they're much harder to separate—and they don't need to be separated to be done effectively.

(You've probably guessed that the same is true for setting priorities—it's part of planning and organizing.)

Setting Priorities

Setting priorities is another aspect of structuring. Most workgroups receive more projects than they can handle in the time available. To succeed, they have to finish the important jobs first and do the rest as time permits.

Raymond Bernstein thought his workgroup was having trouble setting its priorities. He called an informal staff meeting, and this is what he told them:

"First of all, I want each one of you to understand that there's a big difference between 'pressing' and 'important.' A job that's pressing is one that needs to be completed soon—but it may or may not be important. There are also jobs that are important, and they may or may not be pressing. Sometimes it's easy to put off working on an important job because a less important one is pressing. Don't do it unless you're sure that the important one will still get done on schedule.

"Second, no priority is cast in cement—even if I'm the one who set it. If I give you a job and a deadline that you think will make you miss a more important deadline, you need to tell me this *right away*. Then we can decide which project is more important, and I can defend the decision to my boss if necessary.

"Third, never change a priority or deadline at the last minute unless you have a very good reason. If I give you a deadline on something and you come to me the day it's due and say you won't have it done because something more important came up—you're in trouble. It's true, I said you can always negotiate with me if you think a priority's date is unrealistic, but you do this up front, not the day the work is due.

"Finally, you should always know what your most important job is, and that's the job you should be doing. You can always find a few piddling jobs lying around, and every so often you have to do some cleaning up. You can take a little time for this but make sure you don't make it a priority.

"Let me close with a word of wisdom. The difference between an outstanding worker and a so-so worker is not the fact that they do the *same* things, but the outstanding worker does them better. Actually, the outstanding worker does *different* things. Most of the time, this means that he does the most important things—while the so-so worker spends a lot of time on less important things. I want you all to be outstanding workers."

EXAMPLE: Setting Priorities Effectively

Ray calls Kim, one of his newer workers, into his office. "Kim, I want you to take this report and rework the figures in it—using this month's totals. I need it by tomorrow afternoon."

"I can do that, but I'll have to let the cost report slide another day. I'm supposed to have it out on Friday, and if I lose a day, I can't make it."

"Hm, that is a bind."

"Mr. Bernstein, I know how the cost report is used. What are they going to do with this report?"

"Good—I was hoping you'd ask that. Mr. Dubois wants to see how we did this month."

"They need the cost report to plan for next month. Shouldn't I get it done first and then do this revision? I can have the revision for you sometime Monday."

"You're sure you can get it done Monday?"

"Pretty sure. If I can't, I can let you know tomorrow. Is that okay?"

"Yes. I'll let Mr. Dubois know we expect to have it for him Monday."

(**WHAT IF** Kim had just agreed to do the job for Ray without asking questions?)

STRUCTURING IN REQUIRED RESPONSIBILITIES

"Dammit, Marge, managing today isn't what it was when I started! We didn't have to worry about EEO and OSHA and hazardous materials and all that garbage. We could concentrate on what we get paid for—getting the production out."

"I didn't think things were really that bad."

"Well, they are. I try to get the work out, and some turkey comes by and tells me I ought to hire more minority workers. No sooner do I get back to work when someone else comes by and asks me when was the last time I checked to see that everybody was wearing safety shoes and what we do with the used cleaning fluid. Then another joker from the head shed wants to know if I've talked with everybody about the Employee Assistance Program. By the time I get them off my back, the day's over."

"I'm sorry to hear that. I guess things must be different in your section. I try to take these programs in stride and work them along with my regular workload."

"What do you mean, 'work them with your regular workload'?"

"Well, whenever someone tells me I've got to support some new program, I give it the old one–two–three–four."

"The old what?"

"The old one–two–three–four:

1. I find out all I can about the program right away. I want to know how it applies to my people and what we do. That way I can figure out how much impact it'll have.

2. I think about how I can make the program work for me. For example, I've been using EEO for months to get personnel to look harder for better candidates for me. If I'm going to support something, I want it to work *for* me—not against me.

3. Once I understand a new program and what my role is, I make it a part of what I do. When the company put in that Employee Assistance Program, I went over it in a couple of group meetings and I made it one of the things I talk about with people during their appraisals. That's how I found out that one of my people was terribly worried about his daughter. I got him into the program, and now his performance is 100 percent improved.

4. If some program starts getting in our way, I make sure my boss knows about it. I don't make excuses for avoiding the program, but I make sure he knows that it's having a negative impact on morale or productivity or whatever. When they sent out that letter about sexual harassment on the job a few months ago, my guys were almost afraid to talk to the women in the group. Well, I said something to the boss and he talked to the front office, and they sent out that second letter. My people are still a little uneasy, but at least they can talk about it now.

"Anyway, that's my old one–two–three–four. (1) I find out about the program; (2) I make it work for me; (3) I make it a part of what I do on the job; and (4) I let people know if it starts to get in the way. I tell you, it works."

"Ah, you're just lucky, Marge. Besides, you're a woman and they treat you differently anyway. Two more years and you can have this place. . . ."

EXAMPLE: Using Required Programs Effectively

When Marge took over her section, she knew she'd have to pay attention to EEO. Bill, who had had the section before her, had told her that he'd been constantly hassled to hire more minorities. Bill also told her that he would have done so, if he could have found qualified candidates.

One of Marge's first trips was to talk to the EEO manager to make sure she understood how the program worked. Then she made a trip to the personnel office to find out exactly how recruiting was handled.

As a result, she and personnel agreed that they would focus on finding qualified women and minority group candidates for her to consider whenever she had a vacancy. She also made sure that personnel knew she was serious and not just going through the motions.

Because of this action, the EEO manager gave her some slack. Personnel did its job, and when she filled her next five vacancies, she selected one woman and two male members of minority groups. She didn't do anything special—they were just well qualified and available and she picked them.

Marge has been in the job three years now, and no one has hassled her about EEO.

(WHAT IF the workgroup had been having too many accidents when Marge took over? What could she have done to start structuring safety into the way she managed?)

Why are we talking about required programs in this chapter? If you boil down what Marge said, it means "take these programs and *structure* them into your everyday managing." She planned for them, then organized the way they were used, and gave them the priority they needed. And that's what works.

A QUICK SUMMARY

Successful managers are effective at structuring their workgroups. They don't want to waste precious time fighting their workloads.

They *plan,* by

1. Getting all of the intelligence they can so they're not surprised by a change in workload,
2. Keeping up with the status of all the work in their groups,
3. Being realistic when they plan, and
4. Never letting people "fall in love" with the specifics of their plans.

They *organize, by*

1. Starting with a good plan,
2. Having the right people do the right things,
3. Knowing the status of a job at all times, and
4. Seeing that everyone concerned with the job knows who's going to do what.

They *set priorities,* by

1. Knowing the difference between what's pressing and what's important,
2. Letting each worker question even the priorities they impose,
3. Not letting their workers wait until the last minute to change deadlines, and
4. Seeing that their people always know what their most important jobs are and that they work these jobs.

   (And they know that outstanding workers are often outstanding because they get their priorities straight.)

They *deal with a required program,* by

1. Finding out about the program,
2. Making it work for them,
3. Structuring it into what they do on the job, and
4. Letting *their* managers know if the program starts to get in the way of their group's effectiveness.

StretchMeter 2: STRUCTURING

1. Before I make plans, I get all of the information I can.

NEVER   0   1   2   3   4   5   6   7   8   ALWAYS

2. My plans are realistic and practical.

NEVER   0   1   2   3   4   5   6   7   8   ALWAYS

3. My plans make it easy to organize the work.

NEVER   0   1   2   3   4   5   6   7   8   ALWAYS

4. When I organize a project, everyone knows what to do.

NEVER   0   1   2   3   4   5   6   7   8   ALWAYS

5. I can tell the difference between "pressing" and "important."

NEVER   0   1   2   3   4   5   6   7   8   ALWAYS

6. I don't let workers extend deadlines at the last moment.

NEVER   0   1   2   3   4   5   6   7   8   ALWAYS

7. My workers know what their most important jobs are.

NEVER   0   1   2   3   4   5   6   7   8   ALWAYS

8. I understand EEO, safety, and other special programs.

NEVER   0   1   2   3   4   5   6   7   8   ALWAYS

9. I structure these programs into my daily management.

NEVER   0   1   2   3   4   5   6   7   8   ALWAYS

10. I make EEO, safety, etc., work for me and my workgroup.

NEVER   0   1   2   3   4   5   6   7   8   ALWAYS

Structuring ASAP

Which number did you score yourself lowest on in the StretchMeter? Find the ASAP with the same number and do the ASAP starting tomorrow. (And it's okay to do more than one!)

1. Almost every effective management action is based on good information. Get all the facts you can about the next work your unit will get (it can be the morning's work, a new project, or an estimate of something weeks away). Write the information down and use it to plan how you'll handle the workload.

2–3. If your plans aren't realistic and practical, or if they don't make it easy to organize, they won't help much. Write a plan for how you'll spend your morning. Do you spend it that way? If not, plan the afternoon. Keep on planning until you come up with a realistic plan you can stick with; then continue planning every day until it becomes routine.

4. Assigning tasks is a basic part of organizing. Take a plan you're working on now or start a new plan. Write down every task that has to be done. Beside each task, write the name of the person who will do it. If more than one person will do it, identify the person with overall responsibility. See that the job is done that way. Then evaluate how effective you were and do better on the next one.

5. Other people often try to make you think that their pressing deadlines should be important deadlines for you. To be effective in your job, you need to know the difference. Make a list of your workgroup's priorities. Mark each one **P** (for pressing) or **I** (for important). If a task has to be done in the next week, but its completion won't affect your service to your customers or your boss, it's a **P**. If it *will* affect your service to them, no matter when it's due, mark it **I**. If it's an **I** that must be done in the next week, underline it. Do the underlined **I**'s now. Then start on the rest.

6. There is no excuse for deadlines slipped at the last moment, except simple sloppiness. Make it clear to your workers that—unless there is a real emergency—they cannot change a due date without

at least three days' notice. (If three days isn't reasonable for your operation, pick a period of time that is.)

7. Workers should always know which tasks are the most important. Make a list of the jobs in your workgroup, in priority order. Talk with one of your most experienced workers and at least two of the least experienced ones. Ask them what their priorities are. If they aren't almost the same as yours, decide how to communicate more effectively starting today.

8. If you don't understand programs you're required to support, they'll keep getting in your way. Go to the EEO office, the safety office, the Employee Assistance Program office, or a similar office tomorrow morning. Ask the individual responsible for the program to explain how it can help you. Take at least one suggestion and implement it when you get back to your group. (If you can't go there, call.)

9. The way you use required programs effectively is to make them part of your daily managing. Sit down right now and choose at least one way you can use EEO, safety, the Employee Assistance Program, or a similar program as part of your normal routine. Start doing it today.

10. How do you make required programs work for you? See ASAP 8.

CHAPTER 5

Selecting

PHASE ONE MANAGEMENT	
Structuring	C
Selecting	O
Guiding	M
Correcting	M
Motivating	U
Delegating	N
Supporting	I
	C
	A
	T
	I
	N
	G

In this chapter, you'll find useful information on:

What three characteristics the workers you select should have.

How to make effective personnel selections (including how to use interviews to your best advantage).

Why you need to be the kind of manager who will attract high-quality candidates for a job opening.

To develop successful workers, you must select individuals with the potential to be successful. The higher their potential, the less time and effort it will take to develop them.

WHAT IS EFFECTIVE SELECTING?

Henry Montoya is the envy of the other supervisors in the purchasing branch. Somehow he always gets the cream of the crop of new workers. They learn their jobs quickly, do them without a lot of supervision, and seem to enjoy working there.

It's not that Henry hasn't explained.

"Look," he says, "I put time into making my selections. I interview all of the candidates personnel will send me and I study them—carefully. If a person's going to work with us, I want that person to pass three tests:

"First, he has to be able to do the job, or at least be able to learn it quickly.

"Next, I look for motivation. I don't want someone who is going to want to do a good job only if I'm hanging over him all the time.

"Last of all, I look to see if he will fit in—which is really two things: One, I want someone who's going to be happy doing this kind of work day in and day out; and two, I want someone who's going to fit into the workgroup.

"If I can't find someone who can pass all three of these tests, I keep looking. When I do find someone, that's whom I hire. That's really all there is to it."

WHY IS EFFECTIVE SELECTING IMPORTANT?

Some supervisors do a "quick and dirty" job on their selections. Henry knows better. He knows that effective selecting is the basis for everything else he'll do with that worker.

He knows that a new person who doesn't have the right skills will require a lot of extra guiding and correcting.

He knows that a new person who isn't motivated will take extra guiding and correcting, even one who has the skills. Henry's had too much experience to believe that he can "motivate" just anyone. He also knows that it's very time-consuming even when such motivation is successful.

And he knows that a new person who doesn't fit the job and the workgroup, no matter how skilled and motivated he is, will get unhappy with the work sooner or later.

HOW DO I MAKE EFFECTIVE SELECTIONS?

Be Realistic

Always make the best selections possible. But be realistic.

Eleanor Downs is another supervisor who makes excellent selections. But she has a slightly different approach. If she's hiring from outside the organization, she knows her choices are limited by the organization's reputation, the quality of its pay and benefits, any competitors for employees, and a host of other influences she can't control.

It's not much different when she's hiring from inside. Here, she's limited by the selections other supervisors have made, the existing commitments the organization's workers have to it, career patterns, and similar elements that are beyond her control.

Eleanor knows she'll be selective, but she's realistic about how selective she can be. She always tries to get the best available workers, but also knows she may have to compromise at some point and take someone who can't pass all three tests.

If she has to compromise, though, she knows it won't be on motivation. She looks for motivation first, and for the ability to fit in second. If a person passes those two tests, and has the native intelligence her work requires, Eleanor hires him—confident that he will be able to learn to do the job.

EXAMPLE: Realistic Selection

Eleanor learned the hard way about being realistic. Just after she was promoted into her current job, one of the engineers left. She recruited for his replacement for six months without finding someone who was just what she wanted. She finally gave up and took an individual with the right credentials but a poor work history.

Her new engineer was qualified on paper, but he certainly wasn't motivated to do a good job. After spending a lot of time trying to change his attitude, she finally decided to let him go. The day before she planned to tell him, he announced that he had a new job.

Fortunately, Eleanor learned two lessons from the experience. First, she wasn't going to be able to get a top candidate each time. Second, hiring someone who lacked the desire to do a good job was about the worst choice she could make.

She didn't solve the problem completely, but she found ways to reduce it. When the engineer left, she changed the position to that of technician. It turned out that the organization was competitive for technicians, and she hired a good one. In a few months, she had persuaded him to take advantage of the organization's tuition assistance program, and so begin work on an engineering degree at night.

In other words, she's become realistic about making the best selections possible under the circumstances.

(**WHAT IF** engineers suddenly became available on the job market? Should Eleanor keep trying to hire technicians? Remember, you pay technicians less than you pay engineers.)

Eleanor knows, too, about the risk involved in making a selection. There's always the chance that the person she picks won't live up to her expectations. Although this hasn't happened to her yet, she never forgets that it could. Eleanor keeps polishing her selection skills—because she knows that the better she gets at selecting, the better her selections will be.

Gather Lots of Information

One way you keep your mistakes few and far between is to get and use lots of information on the candidates for your jobs.

Robert Stinson knows this, and his selections show it. When he has a job to fill, he takes the time and patience to get the information he needs. He looks at résumés, talks to people, interviews candidates. He knows it would be easier to just hire any candidate who will do. But Robert won't take the easy way out because he knows he'll pay for that mistake a dozen times over.

Instead, Robert concentrates on finding good information. He looks over résumés, evaluations, and any other papers carefully. He may talk with the personnel office about the candidates. But these aren't his main sources. When he really wants the straight scoop, he talks with:

1. The candidate's previous supervisors if he knows and trusts them, especially if they understand his kind of work; and

2. Current or past workers who know the candidate, particularly if they are (were) very good workers.

He's learned to be very suspicious of:

1. Appraisals or ratings that were prepared for the candidate to use for this job, and

2. Written references the candidate brings with him.

    (He knows that supervisors tend to give inflated appraisals of workers in both these situations.)

3. The recommendations of current supervisors he doesn't know (some supervisors will try to "sell" a worker they want to get rid of or talk down a good worker they want to keep).

EXAMPLE: Getting and Using Information

Robert's care saved him on a recent selection. The personnel office sent him a carpenter who had a fine recommendation from her last company. Robert made a routine phone call to her last manager. Sure enough, the candidate's ex-boss was very high in his praise of the woman. He assured Robert that he'd hire her back at any time. When Robert asked if she were leadership material, the other man hesitated—but then assured him energetically that she was.

Robert had the feeling that he shouldn't stop there. He called the woman's manager from her next-to-last job and got a completely different picture. The woman was very competent, the manager said, but he had let her go because of carelessness. In fact, he told Robert, he had heard that she had just had to resign from a job for the same reason.

So, Robert kept on looking.

(**WHAT IF** Robert had told the carpenter he would hire her and then found out about her carelessness? What could he have done then?)

Beware of Your Hot (and Cold) Buttons

Pushing the "hot button" is a phrase salesmen use to describe the positive emotional reaction people have when someone else says or does just the right thing.

Richard Feldman is a new manager who worries about his hot (and cold) buttons a lot. His first two selections turned sour on him. When he reviewed those decisions, he realized that he didn't look carefully enough at either person. Instead, he selected them because they both "seemed" right for the job.

Richard won't do that again. Like the rest of us, he was provided with a generous supply of hot and cold buttons as he was growing up. Now, though, Richard is aware that his buttons were pushed by the people he selected. They appealed to him because they looked like "clean-cut, solid Americans"; perhaps they were, but they turned out to be lousy workers.

Richard has made it a point to get to know and understand his *stereotypes* (another word for hot and cold buttons), and to keep people from using them to manipulate him. Now when he sits across the table from a "clean-cut, solid American," he makes sure that he looks beyond the person's front.

It's paid off for him, too. His third selection was beginning to go the way of the first two, until he asked himself some tough questions. In the end, he selected a minority woman candidate—Velma Thompson—the first woman in his workgroup. She turned out to be one of his best workers.

(Richard had always prided himself on not being discriminatory. If he didn't have any women in his workgroup, he had told himself, it was because none of them had been "well-enough qualified." It shook him to realize how close he had come to deciding that Velma wasn't qualified.)

EXAMPLE: Hot and Cold Buttons

Richard wasn't alone in making mistakes because someone pushed his "hot buttons." We each have a hot or cold button wherever we have accepted the idea that a person who has one characteristic *must* have certain others. These are some examples:

If she's Jewish, then she's good with money.

If he has long hair, he can't be a "solid citizen."

If he looks you in the eye, he can't be lying.

If she has young children, she'll want too much time off.

If he wears a three-piece suit, he can't be a good researcher.

If she's that feminine, she *can't* be an effective boss.

Sometimes each of these is true; sometimes they're false. But when you believe they're always true, you set yourself up to be manipulated:

He wears a business-like haircut and conservative suit—hoping you won't push too hard to find out how little auditing experience he's really had.

Her résumé emphasizes the college she graduated from and her memberships in posh clubs—so you won't look closely at the number of jobs she's held in just three years.

And so it goes.

(**WHAT IF** you're really impressed with a candidate, but during the interview you suddenly push one of his cold buttons? What do you do then?)

Use Interviews Carefully

Interview, but don't put too much faith in the interview.

Marilyn Chan has always been systematic about things. Before she made her first selection as a supervisor, she read several books on interviewing. She wasn't surprised to find that researchers have been studying interviews for decades. But she was surprised to find out how unreliable interviews can be.

What Marilyn discovered was something she really already knew: Candidates don't present honest, unvarnished pictures of themselves in interviews. They try to "sell" themselves and they try to "psyche out" the interviewer by saying exactly what he wants to hear.

Marilyn decided, like most managers, that she still wanted to interview the best-qualified candidates for her jobs. To get the most from her interviews, she decided she would use them to

1. *Obtain information she couldn't easily get otherwise.* Does the candidate sound like he really understands the unit's work? What does he think it would be like to work in Marilyn's kind of work-group?

2. *Observe behavior similar to that which the job requires.* If Marilyn is looking for good people skills, she can judge how well the candidate handles the interview with her. If she needs someone good at communicating, she can evaluate how clearly the candidate explains things to her and how well he listens to what Marilyn says.

3. *Discover how the individual handled certain situations in the past.* What did he do when the computer went down on the night shift? How did he structure his personnel management course? Marilyn is very careful to ask what the person *did*, not what the person *would do*. She knows how easy it is to talk about a brilliant solution and how hard it is to really come up with one when you're on the spot.

EXAMPLE: Effective Interviewing

Marilyn is interviewing the three best candidates for her current vacancy. Each of them could do the job—she's fairly sure of that—but she's not sure which one would do it best.

She reads through their applications and tries to identify any missing information:

> "Says he processed claims fully—did he authorize payment on his own signature?"
>
> "She states that her degree is in business—what courses did she take?"
>
> "I don't understand why he left that job in 1983—need to ask him."

Then Marilyn asks herself what she can learn in the interviews about their behavior. Most of her section's work is done over the phone, so how the candidates dress isn't significant. She decides to pay special attention to how they respond to her questions. Providing complete answers to client inquiries is an extremely important part of the job she's filling.

Finally, she makes a list of problem situations that each of the candidates may have encountered when dealing with clients. For example:

1. "Have you ever had to work with a very distrustful client? How did you handle the situation?"
2. "Please think of the last time you had a client who wouldn't let you go. What did you do?"

Now she's prepared to get as much information as possible from each interview.

(**WHAT IF** Marilyn wanted to know how well a candidate understood basic telephone courtesy? How could she find that out?)

Once she decided how to use the interviews, Marilyn set five goals for each interview. She would

1. Be *completely prepared*. She had to know exactly what she wanted from the interview and how she planned to get it. If not, she might fail to get important information—and make a very poor impression on the interviewee.
2. Give the interview her *undivided attention*. Building a good rapport with the candidate is vital, and an interruption at the wrong time can be disastrous. Marilyn would do whatever she could to prevent interruptions: take her phone off the hook, close her door, even hang out a "Do Not Disturb" sign.
3. *Put the person at ease* first. Marilyn remembered all too well her own experience from the year before. The supervisor jumped right into the interview, and she'd stayed on edge the whole time. Most important, she was sure the supervisor had gotten a completely wrong impression of her. She was determined not to do this to someone else.

   Marilyn asked herself how best to put someone at ease in the stressful atmosphere of an interview. Her answer: Start talking about something that is unrelated to the interview and interesting to the other person.
4. *Ask "open-ended" questions*—those that could not be answered with a simple "yes" or "no." Marilyn knew that this technique draws the other person out more and wouldn't telegraph the answer she wanted.

5. *Listen at least 80 percent of the time.* Marilyn realized she couldn't learn much while she was doing the talking. She also suspected that some of the people she would be interviewing would try to keep *her* talking—so *they* wouldn't have to talk as much. They also could use what she said to help slant their own presentations.

EXAMPLE: Open-Ended Questions

These are some questions Marilyn might select (and some she would discard) for interviews:

"What do you like best about your current job?"
not
"Do you like to work with details?"

"What are you looking for in a boss?"
not
"Do you want a boss who lets you take the initiative?"

"Tell me about your typing."
not
"How fast can you type?"

"How do you feel about your progress in your career?"
not
"Are you satisfied with your progress in your career?"

(**WHAT IF** Marilyn wanted to find out if the candidate was truly interested in working for her organization? What kind of question(s) could she ask?)

Become Known as a Good Manager

The final key to good selecting is having the kind of reputation that makes good people want to work for you.

Let's go back to Henry Montoya again. He knows what he's looking for, and he works hard at selecting. He also has something else going for him—something even he doesn't fully realize.

Henry works hard at the kinds of skills this book describes. He develops successful workers. The rest of the organization recognizes that, and his people regularly get selected for promotion. As a result, people are anxious to work for Henry, and he always has top-flight workers applying to fill his jobs.

(Word gets around in an organization. When a manager becomes known as someone who treats people right, develops their skills, and helps them get ahead, good employees want to work for that manager. His selections get even better because now there is a better pool of applicants for each job.)

That's what's happened with Henry. People know that he develops successful workers, and they want to be part of his team. That makes his effective selecting practices even more effective, which results in better selections, who become very successful workers, who attract other good workers, etc. . . . .

In other words, nothing succeeds like success.

A QUICK SUMMARY

The managers described in this chapter know that effective selecting means finding individuals who have the right skills and the proper motivation, and who are good matches with their work and their work-groups.

They know that a candidate who doesn't pass all three tests of a good worker will take a great deal of extra supervisory time and effort to learn the job and stay with it. If they have to accept someone who doesn't meet all their standards, they'll select the candidate with good motivation who is less highly skilled over the one who has great skills but a problem attitude.

They know how to make effective selections. They

1. Are realistic;
2. Gather lots of information about the candidates;
3. Are aware of their hot (and cold) buttons;
4. Use interviews carefully to

   a. Gather information they can't easily get otherwise,

   b. Observe behavior similar to that which the job requires, and

   c. Discover how the candidates handled certain situations in the past.

To be effective in interviews, they know they must

1. Be completely prepared,
2. Give the other person their undivided attention,
3. Put the other person at ease,
4. Ask open-ended questions, and
5. Listen at least 80 percent of the time.

They try to be the kind of manager who attracts high-quality candidates to their workgroups.

StretchMeter 3: SELECTING

1. I'm willing to take the time necessary to make good selections.

NEVER   0   1   2   3   4   5   6   7   8   ALWAYS

2. I know how to effectively gather information on candidates.

NEVER   0   1   2   3   4   5   6   7   8   ALWAYS

3. I can tell when someone pushes one of my hot buttons.

NEVER   0   1   2   3   4   5   6   7   8   ALWAYS

4. I know how to set goals for an interview.

NEVER   0   1   2   3   4   5   6   7   8   ALWAYS

When I interview,[1]

5. I can keep the conversation on the subject I want to discuss.

NEVER   0   1   2   3   4   5   6   7   8   ALWAYS

6. I can give the other person my complete attention.

NEVER   0   1   2   3   4   5   6   7   8   ALWAYS

7. I know how to put the other person at ease quickly.

NEVER   0   1   2   3   4   5   6   7   8   ALWAYS

8. I ask open-ended questions.

NEVER   0   1   2   3   4   5   6   7   8   ALWAYS

9. I'm able to listen at least 80 percent of the time.

NEVER   0   1   2   3   4   5   6   7   8   ALWAYS

---

[1] If you don't have direct interviewing experience, rate yourself on items 5 through 8 in terms of your general conversation skills.

Selecting ASAP

1. If you haven't been willing to take the time you need to make good selections, you may still have the idea that what's important is the "work" that you do. You need to remember that selecting is one of the seven critical activities of Phase One Management. If you keep that clearly in mind, you'll soon be taking the time you need.

2. Effectively gathering information can be difficult, but it's absolutely essential. This tip will help you do it: Pick out your two or three best workers and your two or three poorest (if you have any). Get their personnel files. Go through their employment information and see if you could have predicted what kind of workers they would be from the records. (Even if you can't, you should have a clearer idea of what to look for in the future.)

3. It's not very difficult to tell when a hot (or cold) button has been pushed. When you have a strong positive or negative reaction to someone or something based on one or a few of his or its characteristics, that's a button. Use a Reaction Alert like the one described in the ASAP for Chapter 1 to keep track of how many times this happens in, say, a week. When you start paying attention in this way, you'll start to see patterns in your reactions. The clearer the patterns become, the easier it will be to protect yourself against them.

4. You must have well-thought-out, realistic goals for an interview if you want it to be successful. For practice, prepare to interview three candidates for a vacancy. If you have a real vacancy, great. If not, imagine that you're interviewing three workers—in your own or another workgroup—that you know only slightly. Write down what you want to know about each candidate when the interview is over. Then write down what you know about each candidate *now*. The difference between the two lists for each candidate is your goal for that interview.

5. Keeping a conversation on the subject you want to discuss is an easy skill to work on (though not necessarily an easy one to master). Starting tomorrow morning, have a minimum of two conversations per day for a week in which you hold the conversation to a specific

topic for at least five minutes. The more subtly and naturally you can do this, the better. (Hint: One of the best ways to keep a conversation focused where you want it is to keep asking relevant questions.)

6. Paying complete attention to a person you're talking with is a skill that is valuable in many different situations. Copy the pattern in ASAP 5 above: For a week, have a minimum of two conversations a day in which you concentrate completely on the other person for at least five minutes. If you rated yourself low in #5 also, you can combine the two in the same conversations.

7. It would be a shame to do everything else right and then have the interview fail because the person you were interviewing couldn't loosen up. Within the next week, create a list of at least ten conversation topics that could be used to break the ice. One method is to listen to other people talking and to write down some of the topics they discuss in a relaxed and enthusiastic way. Test your list by talking about a topic with others—preferably people you've just met. Replace any of the topics that don't work well. Now you have a list of topics to use to open interviews.

8. Asking effective, open-ended questions is one of the most useful skills you can have. For the next week, carry your counter with you. Count each time you ask a question that can be answered with a "yes" or a "no." By how much can you reduce your daily count in a week? The second week, count each open-ended question you ask. How much can you increase this total?

9. Being a good listener is another valuable skill (and one that will be discussed again in this book). For the next week, pick at least one conversation a day in which you will listen no less than 80 percent of the time. Do it. If possible, have someone who knows what you're trying to do listen to the conversation—then ask him if you actually listened as much as you thought you did. Typically, each of us believes that we listen more than an outside observer believes we do. If that's the case with you, change it.

CHAPTER 6

Guiding

PHASE ONE MANAGEMENT	
Structuring	C
Selecting	O
Guiding	M
Correcting	M
Motivating	U
Delegating	N
Supporting	I
	C
	A
	T
	I
	N
	G

In this chapter, you'll find useful information on:

> Seeing that workers know *what to do.*
>
> Making sure that they know *how to do it well.*
>
> Ensuring that the workers understand the importance of quality.
>
> Paying special attention to workers who have just made major transitions.

This chapter will provide you with the tools you need to begin developing workers who know *what to do* and *how to do it well.*

WHAT IS EFFECTIVE GUIDING?

Lee Chen learned the hard way how important effective guiding is. When he first came to America, he spoke almost no English. He'll never forget how difficult it was to adapt to a new culture, get a job, and learn to speak English, all at the same time. Lee remembers the people who were patient with him while he was learning, and those who weren't.

Now Lee is a manager. Most of the people he selects already speak English and most of them know something about the work of the section. But Lee still concentrates on guiding them carefully until they learn everything they need to know to be successful workers.

One of Lee's top priorities is making sure that each new worker knows *what to do*. He carefully outlines what the section does and explains each of the deadlines that must be met. Then he explains why each job is necessary. After a week or two, Lee sends each new worker to visit the section that uses the reports he creates, and has the manager of that section explain the purpose of those reports.

Next, Lee concentrates on seeing that each new employee knows *how to do his job well*. Lee assigns the person to one of his senior employees who knows how to get the job done efficiently and well. During the training, Lee talks frequently with the trainers, making sure that they're patient and encouraging with new workers.

There's one point that Lee repeats over and over to each new worker: "We have to do high quality work. I want you to learn to work with great efficiency, and I want you to perform tasks on time—*but* I want you to do them right the first time. We are too busy to spend time doing work over again."

WHY IS EFFECTIVE GUIDING IMPORTANT?

Ask Julia Szabo, she'll tell you:

"When I started in this job, I though it was best to allow people to pick things up on their own. 'It lets them show initiative,' I said. Boy, was I wrong! They may have had initiative, but it took forever for them to learn to do things properly.

"That's when I changed my tactics. Now I let my best people train the new ones because they enjoy doing it. But I check to make sure that the new workers are learning what I want them to learn. I work with the new people also, just to reassure myself. My new system works; the new workers learn the job faster, and they do it better.

"I also found it was a good way for all of us to get to know the new person. Working with him conveys the feeling that we all care about his performance. And we get a better sense of what the person is like, and what we need to emphasize in his training.

"Something else is important. It's easy to fall into the habit of only paying attention to people when they foul up, which is a negative way of managing. Putting some time and energy into guiding your workgroup turns this around. I get used to helping them, and my people start to see me more as a coach than a boss. It's easier now for me to correct them, and they're more honest with me when they have a problem.

"There's one other thing I should mention. Most of the people in my section started in this department right after college. A couple of years ago, though, we began promoting some clerks from other departments. At first it didn't look like things were going to work out—and then I suddenly realized what the problem was. The new people didn't understand how what we do is different from what clerks do. They were trying to do our job, but they were looking at it as a clerical job.

"As soon as I understood, I began working with them to show them how the jobs differed. One of them just couldn't get it, but the others have turned out to be excellent workers. I think the moral of this is that when a job represents a big change for someone, you must take extra care to see that he's guided properly."

HOW DO I GUIDE EFFECTIVELY?

Harold Taplinger is a graduate student in business school. As part of a course assignment, he's talking with Lee and Julia about how they became so effective at guiding their employees. This is part of their conversation:

Guiding New Workers

Harold: Do both of you use senior workers to train new workers?

Lee: I introduce the new person to everyone in the unit and talk about what we do and why it is done. Then I turn him over to my senior workers for training. I keep up with the person's progress, though, and I guide him myself on the things I think are most important.

Julia: That's what I had been doing, too. We're trying something a little different now. I sent my two top people to an on-the-job training course, and they're going to be our official "tutors" for the new people. We've prepared a training manual that outlines what a new worker needs to know, and the tutors will use it. I will stay involved enough to get to know each person and establish a coaching relationship with him.

Harold: Have you tried out your "tutoring" system yet?

Julia: We're right in the middle of our first trial now. I'm not certain yet, but it looks like it's working well.

Lee: I have thought of trying Julia's way, but the members of my group get such pleasure from working with new people that they all want to take part and help. They like to work as a team, and I have been afraid to do anything that might interfere with that.

EXAMPLE: Guiding New Workers

Bilal has just come to work for Julia. She sets aside an hour at the beginning of his first day to talk with him and find what he needs to learn to do his new job successfully.

She already knows from his application that he's done the same work for two other organizations. During their conversation, she learns that his skills are well developed but that the other organizations' procedures were very different. She decides that he needs to learn her workgroup's procedures first.

Fortunately, the workgroup has several jobs needing analysis that are good training material for Bilal. Julia calls in Winston, one of her most experienced workers. She explains to him that she wants Bilal to analyze the jobs, with Winston to help him. She makes it clear that Bilal has the skills, and Winston's job is to show him the procedures he should use.

Julia asks Winston to start by helping Bilal identify which factors should be used in analyzing the first two jobs. Then she asks them both to get back to her so that Bilal can explain why he selected those factors. This will give her a clearer idea of how much training Bilal will need, and it will also help her get to know him a little better.

(**WHAT IF** Bilal lacks several important skills? How should Julia start him out?)

Sharing Skills

Lee: Let me tell you about something I have begun with my experienced workers. For a long time, I had believed that some of them were just naturally better workers than others. Then I watched one of my very good workers help another one, and that one really improved. It started me thinking, and then I began asking workers with a recognized skill to demonstrate it for the others. It is having some good results.

Julia: What about the ones you don't ask to demonstrate? Don't they get put out?

Lee: I have been lucky because I have been able to find something for each person to talk about. Even our newest worker developed something that the others had not discovered. They all have tremendous enthusiasm now for helping each other.

Julia: I've also noticed how some workers like to pass on their skills. Now that my people all know each other well, some of the best workers voluntarily help others with difficult jobs. In fact, I've just appointed someone in the group who isn't a tutor to be the official "helper." She was very pleased and suggested several skills she thought she could share with others.

Harold: Some teachers say that everyone can be taught to do a job as well as the best person. It sounds like you'd agree.

Lee: I do not know if it applies to everyone, but I have seen workers improve greatly by learning from others.

Julia: I have, too. I believe that most people really want to do a good job, and I think it's important to be patient with them and encourage them to help each other. That's one reason why I like the word "guide." I'd rather think of myself as a guide than a "boss" or a "know-it-all."

Harold: Yes, but don't you have to "chew out" workers, too?

Lee: I do not find that necessary very often. Besides, I believe that that topic will be covered in the next chapter.

EXAMPLE: Sharing Skills

At first, Lee wants his most skilled workers to start sharing their best skills with the others right away. As he thinks more about it, though, he realizes there are potential problems. His workgroup hasn't worked together long enough to completely trust each other. He's afraid that those who need to develop their skills might feel insulted by the demonstrations.

So, Lee waits for a while. He arranges things so that different workers get the opportunity to work closely with each other, which builds up the trust he needs. It also gives the workers a chance to see just how skilled some of the others are. In fact, he notices several times that one of them will ask another to share a specific skill.

Several months pass. Then Lee gets his chance during a group meeting, when Amy thanks John for showing her a particularly good shortcut.

"I think each of us has something to share with the others," Lee says. "I would like to have a meeting every other Friday and turn the meeting over to a different person each time. I want that person to select what he feels is his best skill and explain it to the others. How do you feel about that?"

A few workers hesitate, but most of them are willing to try it. Lee sets the first meeting up with Rafael leading it. Because Rafael is well known as the most skilled worker in the group, Lee thinks no one will be embarrassed to learn from him.

They aren't, and the session goes very well. After that, everyone is enthusiastic about the idea.

(**WHAT IF** Lee wanted to start the program, but no one gave him an opening? How could he have initiated it in that situation?)

The Importance of Quality

Julia: Can I change the subject a little? We haven't talked at all about quality, and I think quality is very important.

Harold: My professors are saying that American companies must improve their quality if we're to be competitive internationally.

Julia: I don't know about internationally, but I know that my people *want* to produce high quality. I think most workers do. When I started with a manufacturing outfit across town years ago, we didn't have much competition, and what we built was pretty sloppy. And the people who worked there hated that! I've never been anywhere that the morale was so low, and the poor work they put out was the primary cause.

Lee: I know. When I became a first-level manager, nearly a third of the workers in my section were spending most of their time reviewing the others' work. What they meant by "reviewing" was inspecting. We have changed that, and now everybody feels better. And we have increased the work we do and the quality of it. Inspecting is a very inefficient way to get quality work.

Julia: Yes. I think my people get tired of hearing me say "Do it right the first time," but I keep on saying it. I want them to *expect* to get it right without anyone else having to look at it.

Harold: Some books call that "conformance to requirements."

Lee: I believe it is better to speak of conforming to what the people who use our products expect. These are really our "customers," and we need to produce what they want. Once every three months I take several of my people and we meet with some workers from the unit that uses what we produce. We want to make sure that we are giving them what they desire and that we are giving it to them the first time.

Julia: Yes, I do the same thing, but not on a regular schedule. We've made quite a few changes because of what our "customers" have told us. The importance of doing quality work is emphasized to my people. I'm also going to do something else I think is exciting. Marketing has agreed to let three of my people sit in on its next focus group so that they can see what customers do with the information we research.

EXAMPLE: Improving Quality

Paul finds that he has a quality problem on the day he takes over the Routine Claims Section.

This section receives each routine health insurance claim and decides what payment should be made. After a claims clerk has made the decision, the claim moves to the Claims Payment Section next door. There, an authorization clerk reviews the decision before payment is made.

When Paul looks at the statistics for the previous week, he's shocked. Fifteen percent of the decisions made by the claims clerks were turned back by the authorization clerks and had to be redone.

Paul talks informally with the claims clerks about the situation. He finds that they

1. Resent having the authorization clerks check their work,
2. Often don't worry about doing sloppy work because they know it will be caught and they can redo it, and
3. Feel that the authorization clerks "ought to have to work hard because they get paid more than we do."

Paul realizes that the current situation is wasting a great deal of time and effort, and making everyone angry in the process. In the long run, he plans to work with the supervisor of the Payment Section to develop cooperation between the two units. But he wants to produce some improvement right away.

Paul would like to post each clerk's error rate but is afraid that will just make them angrier. In talking to the clerks, he finds that most of them want to be promoted to the Nonroutine Claims Section—but that their section's reputation keeps most of them from even being considered for openings there.

Paul has found what he's looking for. He persuades the Nonroutine Claims Section supervisor to give a two-hour training session on processing difficult claims every other Friday afternoon. Then he sets the policy that any clerk who holds his error rate down to five percent or less for two weeks can attend the training session.

It starts slowly, but before too long every clerk's error rate is under five percent. The clerks are enthusiastic about the training sessions, but something more important happens: They begin to feel better about themselves and their work—and the Payment Section begins to feel better about them.

There's even another benefit: Because the clerks feel better about their work, they aren't as defensive when Paul makes suggestions for improving it.

(WHAT IF Paul's next step is to reduce the error rate to two percent or less? How could he do it?)

Guiding Workers in Transition

Julia: Harold, there's one other thing we need to talk about—managing workers who're making major transitions.

Harold: I'm not quite sure what you mean by "major transitions."

Julia: Well, most people who come into my jobs are pretty well prepared for them. We have to teach them the specifics of the jobs but they learn them quickly. This isn't always true, though. We've promoted a number of clerks in the last few years, and it has been a big transition for them to move from clerical to analytical work.

Harold: Do you mean they weren't able to do it?

Julia: No—once they understood the difference, they learned very well. But my experienced workers and I had to spend a lot of time making the difference clear to them.

Lee: It is not just clerks. When I became a first-level manager, no one explained to me what a big change that was. I kept trying to do the work along with my people. We got into a very large mess before I learned that my job was now something very different.

Julia: I had that problem, too. And there are many other situations where people have to make big jumps. It's tough for someone who is on his first job, or for someone coming back to work after raising a family.

Lee: Yes, and it is very hard to go from a job out in the plant to one in the offices here. I can also tell you that it is difficult when you feel like an outsider. In my case, that was language and not knowing American culture, but it can be many things.

Julia: I know. I was the first female manager here, and I felt like an outsider for quite a while.

Harold: Let me make sure I understand this—because it's new to me. You're saying that you have to be particularly careful when you're guiding workers who've made a major career move. These are people who've moved into very different kinds of work, or who're working for the first time or returning to work after several years off. Also, people from different ethnic groups or backgrounds, who may feel strange in the workgroup, need extra attention. Is that right?

(Julia nods.)

EXAMPLE: Transitional Workers

Arlene is the first clerk to be promoted to job analyst in Julia's branch. She started as a records clerk and then worked her way up to senior clerk in the training section. Because she's very intelligent and gets along extremely well with other people, Julia selected her as a trainee analyst.

Although Arlene tries hard, she just isn't catching on to the work. Several of the other analysts complain to Julia that they have to explain things over and over to her, and even then, she often doesn't understand. Everybody likes her, but they are running out of patience.

Julia makes it a point to work with Arlene herself. She finds that Arlene keeps asking her questions instead of using her own judgment. She mentions this to Arlene once; the woman gets flustered and upset, and Julia has to break off the discussion.

Julia doesn't want to give up on Arlene because she remembers how hard it was when she became the first female manager in the division. One day, as she's driving home from work, she suddenly realizes what the problem is.

Julia talks with Arlene the next day and confirms her thought. Arlene was working in a job where her function was to apply rules. Arlene's greatest skill, in fact, is that she can identify and apply very complicated rules. But they're still rules. She has no experience at analyzing a situation—which is a very different mental skill.

Julia starts to work with Arlene on basic analytic skills and sends her to a few courses. The going is slow at first, but then Arlene begins to understand the difference. . . .

Two years later, Arlene is the worker assigned to train the new analyst who's just been promoted from a clerical position in the recruiting branch.

(**WHAT IF** Arlene had been an analyst before but had been out of the job market for 15 years to raise a family? What kind of transitional help would she have been most apt to need?)

Harold: Thank you. I think I can write up the heart of what you've said as . . .

A QUICK SUMMARY

1. It's very important to help new people become a part of the workgroup.

2. New workers must know what to do and how to do it well.

3. Doing it well means doing quality work the first time.

4. Managers need to be certain that new workers are learning the right things, whether the managers are teaching the new people themselves or have assigned that responsibility to senior workers.

5. Anyone who trains a new worker should think of himself as a guide or a coach, not a boss or a judge.

6. Managers especially need to pay close attention to people who are making a major transition and provide them with the extra guidance they need.

StretchMeter 4: GUIDING

1. My workers want to do a good job.

NEVER   0   1   2   3   4   5   6   7   8   ALWAYS

2. I help others learn instead of doing the job myself.

NEVER   0   1   2   3   4   5   6   7   8   ALWAYS

3. My workers know what our customers[1] want.

NEVER   0   1   2   3   4   5   6   7   8   ALWAYS

4. My workers know how to do all their tasks well.

NEVER   0   1   2   3   4   5   6   7   8   ALWAYS

5. My workers produce high quality work.

NEVER   0   1   2   3   4   5   6   7   8   ALWAYS

6. I am a coach instead of a boss.[2]

NEVER   0   1   2   3   4   5   6   7   8   ALWAYS

7. I know which of my workers are making major transitions.

NEVER   0   1   2   3   4   5   6   7   8   ALWAYS

8. I give special attention to workers making major transitions.

NEVER   0   1   2   3   4   5   6   7   8   ALWAYS

---

[1]Remember, your customers are those who use whatever you produce. For many workgroups, that's another part of the organization, not the final customer.

[2]This book keeps referring to being a boss as something you want to avoid, but it keeps referring to your "boss"—not your "manager" or your "coach." Here's why:

> If you have an understanding and helpful manager, that's great. If you don't, though, you can't wait for him to change so that you can succeed. He may be a "boss" in all of the worst senses of the word, but he's still *your* boss. He may change, but he hasn't. If you're going to succeed, you're going to do it working for him just as he is now.

Guiding ASAP

1. If you don't believe that your workers want to do a good job most of the time, you're not going to give them proper guidance. Choose a worker you feel certain isn't particularly interested in doing a good job. Think about the last three mistakes he made. Now, how could those mistakes have been caused by not knowing how to do something rather than not wanting to do it? Don't quit until you have an answer to that question (even if you don't believe it's true). For the next week, act as though you think that not knowing is the answer. What happens?

2. Doing things yourself instead of helping others learn to do them is a bad habit—one that calls for a Reaction Alert. (Don't know what that is? See the ASAP for Chapter 1.) Use your Reaction Alert to train yourself to help others learn, as a substitute for your habitual reaction of doing things yourself.[3]

3. To paraphrase an old saying, if your workers don't know what your customers want, it's going to be hard to tell when they've given it to them. Make an appointment now to have someone from the section that uses what you produce, come and talk with your group about how that section uses your output. If you have more than one customer, make plans to have each of them come in and do this—or for your workgroup to visit their areas and see for themselves how your product is used.

4. If your workers don't know how to do all their tasks well, you're wasting their talents. Your first step is to determine what doing a task "well" means. Pick one task—an important one—and locate the worker who does it best. Observe how he does it. Then see that the other workers learn how to do the task that way. Keep it up until

---

[3] I know that Reaction Alerts work for this, because that's what I developed the one on my desk for. Specifically, I wanted to break myself of the bad habit of solving problems for my workers. Because I want them to be successful, I want them to be good at problem solving. My Reaction Alert reminds me not to take their problem away from them and solve it, but to help them understand and solve it themselves.

everyone knows how to do everything well. (Afraid this will take months? Okay, let it take months.)

5. If your workers don't produce high quality work, you have dissatisfied workers—no matter how good everything else is. You can't change the situation overnight with pep talks or by publishing a new policy. But you can pick one process or output that can be measured—today—and start measuring it. When you reduce errors to zero, go on to the next one. WARNING: This is a never-ending process. (Pick an important process or output if you can, but pick one—and begin to improve it.)

6. A boss gets results by *forcing* his workers to do their jobs. A coach gets results by *helping* his workers do their jobs. A successful manager is more coach than boss. If you're spending too much time being a boss, you may believe that your workers don't really *want* to do a good job. Try the exercise in ASAP 1 with the worker you have to boss the most.

7. Even very bright, very motivated workers can have difficulties when they're making a major transition from one job to another (or from not working). Identify someone in your group who is making a major transition and find out how he thinks and feels about it. When you've made yourself aware of the problems he faces, find out tactfully if there are others making a similar transition. (If none of your workers is in transition, see if you can find someone in another workgroup who is, and talk with him to get a better feel for the problems workers encounter in that situation.)

8. It doesn't help to know who's making a major transition if you don't do anything about it. Try the direct approach. Sit down with each person who's making a significant transition and ask him to list the problems as he sees them. Listen carefully, because you may have to hear some of it "between the lines." Once you know what each person's situation is, you can guide him more effectively toward becoming a successful worker.

CHAPTER 7

Correcting

PHASE ONE MANAGEMENT	
Structuring	C
Selecting	O
Guiding	M
Correcting	M
Motivating	U
Delegating	N
Supporting	I
	C
	A
	T
	I
	N
	G

In this chapter, you'll find useful information on:

How important effective positive and negative feedback are for successful performance, especially for new workers.

An effective strategy to use when correcting workers.

The benefits of a system that gives prompt performance feedback directly to workers.

This information will aid you in further developing workers who know what to do and how to do it. It will also assist you in finding ways to ensure that workers know when they've done their jobs well. In turn, this will help your workers become motivated to want to do well.

WHAT IS EFFECTIVE CORRECTING?

R aymond Hill had always thought that the way to improve workers'
performance was to tell people when they weren't doing a good
job.

If his workgroup's reject rate got too high, Ray would call those
workers together and tell them that he expected them to do better. If the
reject rate was particularly bad that week, he made sure that he really
chewed on them. When that didn't work, he tried appealing to their
pride—without any better results. Ray was on the verge of quitting as a
manager, when his organization sent him to a "refresher" course in
management.

"I didn't think what the instructors were saying in the course would
work on the job," Ray admits, "but things were so bad I was willing to
try anything. I was amazed at what happened. I didn't believe it at first,
but I sure believe it now.

"The first thing I found out was that a lot of my people didn't even know
when they were doing things wrong. The pieces they produced went on
to the next section, and if those pieces weren't right, they'd be fixed by
the workers there and marked down on the reject summary that was sent
to me each week. The people in my group who made the mistakes
usually didn't know they were making them. They didn't even know I
was talking to *them* when I yelled about the rejects.

"Then I found that my two best workers were doing something about
this situation on their own. Whenever I really yelled about a bad product,
they'd go over to the next section and ask a worker there to show them
what was wrong. If it was something they had been fouling up, they'd
change it. That way, they stayed out of trouble, but no one else in the
group knew their secret.

"Well, to make a long story short, I made a lot of changes. What they
really amounted to is this:

1. I make sure that every worker knows how *he* is doing. I still get the
    overall reject figure, but I make sure I have a breakdown for each
    individual, too.

2. When someone is making a mistake, I see that he knows about it right
    away. If I wait a week, that worker may produce a bad product for

a week. So, I get the data every evening, and the next morning I discuss any problems with the workers involved.

3. If workers are not producing good products, they also need to know what they have to change to improve. That may sound silly, but I found that most of my people who didn't seem to care, actually didn't know what they'd done wrong, or why it was wrong, or how to do better.

"As a matter of fact, over the past six years I've had only one worker who didn't produce a good product once he knew what he'd done wrong, why it was wrong, and how to do it right."

WHY IS EFFECTIVE CORRECTING IMPORTANT?

Ellie Donahue has been a supervisor for just two years. Before she began this job, she read a book on successful management that emphasized effective correcting. She tried doing what the book suggested, and it worked.

Ellie discovered that quick correction is very important with new workers. If this doesn't happen, they'll learn how to do their jobs incorrectly. New workers need to know when they're doing their jobs *correctly*, too—so they can keep performing that way.

Ellie learned that experienced workers may need correction just as much as new ones. When things just go along and nobody says anything, workers sometimes fall into bad habits and produce sloppy work. She wants to avoid having any of her good workers ruined this way. Ellie's found that when each worker in her group knows how he's doing and knows what Ellie expects from him, this doesn't happen.

HOW DO I CORRECT EFFECTIVELY?

Correcting Is Okay

First of all, as either Ray or Ellie will tell you, correcting is okay—as long as you understand it and use it effectively. It's easy to think of correcting as something negative, such as pointing out to someone that he's wrong.

And many people have painful memories of being harshly "corrected" by their parents and teachers.

"That's not what I mean by 'correcting,' at all," Ellie says. "I try to be very tactful, and I don't correct anyone in front of others. The most important point, though, is that I believe that my workers *want* to do things right. I'm not trying to 'shape them up'; I'm giving them the information they need to do the job the way they want to do it. That's a completely different thing."

Ray continues the theme: "Exactly. A worker who makes a mistake can't correct the mistake until he knows what, why, and how: *What* he did wrong, *why* it was wrong, and *how* to do it right.

"If you give an individual that information and he continues to make mistakes, you may have a problem employee. But when the worker doesn't have this information, the manager is the problem."

"We certainly agree on that," Evelyn adds. "And the worker needs all three pieces of information:

1. When mistakes are made, your worker has to know *what* he didn't do correctly (or well). Without this input, he'll either continue to think the work is acceptable or may completely misunderstand what was wrong.

2. Your worker has to understand *why* it was wrong. People don't usually make mistakes because they lack intelligence. They may leave a step out, or do the steps in the wrong order. They may try to reason out how it ought to be done—but don't know enough to reason correctly. Unless they find out why what they did was wrong, they can't know just what needs to be done to correct it.

3. Finally, your worker has to know *how* to do the job right, which is different from you telling him to do it right. He learns how when you *tell* him what to do, *show* him how to do it, and then watch him *practice* doing it.

"The point is that I think most errors are made because workers don't have enough information to prevent them. Our first responsibility as managers is to see that this doesn't happen with *our* workers."

EXAMPLE: Effective Correcting, I

"Ray, I just don't know about Evelyn Jones. I don't think she's ever going to learn how to set up a jig correctly. I've showed her how three times, and I just had to set it up for her again."

"Hmmm. Does she know that she made a mistake?"

"Sure—I told her."

"Do you know what her mistake was?"

"No—and I don't see what that has to do with it. I showed her how to do it correctly, and I told her when she did it wrong. That ought to be enough! She should have more common sense."

"No, Tony, what you've done isn't enough—and it has nothing to do with common sense. If I'd trained you that way when you first came to work here, I'd still be setting up jigs for *you*. Let's go over there, and I'll show you what I mean."

"Evelyn, Tony tells me you're having a problem setting up your jig when you change runs."

"Yes, Mr. Hill, I am. I don't understand it—I know I'm doing everything Tony tells me to do."

"How about taking it apart and letting me watch you put it back together, okay?" Evelyn nodded. She hesitated a moment, then disassembled the jig and began reassembling it.

"That's it," Ray said. "You're trying to anchor the back before the front of it is set, which prevents the tongue from seating properly. Tony, show her what I mean."

Tony lifted the jig slightly and pointed to the problem. "Oh, I see it now," Evelyn said excitedly.

"Now, Tony, show her how it should be done." He did. "Okay, take it apart again. Evelyn, why don't you try it?" She did, and smiled as parts slid smoothly together.

"Thanks," she said.

"Evelyn, I was just telling Tony how important it is for someone who makes an error to know what the error is, why it is an error, and how to correct it. Tony, are you a believer now?"

Tony grinned sheepishly and nodded.

(**WHAT IF** Ray had just told Evelyn she'd get it if she'd only pay more attention? What do you think would have happened?)

Correcting a Worker

Ellie frowned thoughtfully. "There's another aspect to correcting: It's not always clear whether the worker made a mistake or not. For instance, my group primarily does quick-and-dirty custom work. I don't mean we do sloppy work—we don't. But a lot of what we do is writing short data analysis utilities for some special purpose. A researcher will call us and say he needs to do such-and-such an analysis. One of my programmers will knock something out, give it a quick test, and send it up.

"The problem is that we don't always furnish what the person wanted. Then he complains, and I have to get involved. Before I talk to my programmer, though, I don't know whether the programmer made an error or our customer was unclear about what was needed."

"I see what you're saying," Ray commented. "Most of the time, it's obvious if one of my people makes an error. I get together with him; use the what, why, and how method; and correct the error. But with your group, you have to determine first whether your programmer goofed or your customer failed to describe what he wanted well enough. I can see how that complicates matters."

"It does. When I first took over the section, I really wanted to please our customers. When a customer complained, I leaned on my people. That didn't work very well. The people in my group felt I wasn't supporting them and wasn't interested in their side of the story."

"What did you do?"

"Well, I've worked out a way of correcting that succeeds most of the time. It goes like this: First of all, when I discuss performance with a worker, it's no one else's business. I ask him to join me somewhere where we can talk privately. I'm sure you do that."

Ray nodded emphatically.

"Next, I don't assume that I know what happened. I want to listen to my worker, and I want him to know that I'm willing to listen. That means I spend the time necessary to find out how my worker sees the situation. Sometimes I hear what I expect to hear. Sometimes, though, I find I've gotten the wrong idea—it's important that *I* get corrected, too.

"My goal is for us to discuss the situation until we both see it the same way. It doesn't always happen, but I know that when it does, it makes things a lot easier for us both."

"What if you don't think your worker did anything wrong—what do you do then?"

"That's easy. If I'm satisfied he did a good job, I make sure he knows I'm satisfied. Then I thank him for discussing it with me, and the talk ends there. If I'm not satisfied, if the worker really didn't do what should have been done, I try to let him realize this for himself. If he does, I know we'll be able to correct the problem quickly. When the worker takes responsibility for the problem, I can put all my energy into helping him find a solution.

"You know as well as I do that the worker doesn't always recognize his error, which means that I have to point it out. I do it as objectively as I can; I never make it sound like I've caught him at something or I'm blaming him for something. Unless the worker proves otherwise to me, I figure that he's just as interested in doing a good job as I am in having it done.

"Finally, I make sure that the worker understands exactly what he did wrong, why it was wrong, and how to do it right. If necessary, I go through the tell–show–practice sequence again. I know that different people learn at different speeds, and I don't mind repeating guidance I've already given."

EXAMPLE: Effective Correcting, II

"Jared, I want to talk to you about the data conversion program you did for Dr. Stennis. She says it gives her the wrong answer about a third of the time."

"Yeah, I guess it does. She's using negative fractions, and the conversion routine wasn't designed to handle them. If she'd told me everything she wanted when she first called, this wouldn't have happened."

"What did she say she wanted?"

"She called down in a hurry, like she always does, and said she needed a data converter. I figured she was working with the same kind of problems as Dr. Yankelovich, so I took the converter I did for him and doctored it a little bit."

"You didn't ask her for any details about the data?"

"No, that shouldn't be my job. She's the Ph.D.—she ought to be able to tell me what she wants."

"Maybe so—but wouldn't everybody have been better off if you'd asked her a few questions? I know you're not happy that she thinks you made a mistake."

"No, I'm not. And in answer to your question, it gripes me; but, yes, I should have asked her. The fact that she didn't tell me what she wanted is no excuse for me to turn out something she thinks is wrong. I have more pride than that."

"I know you do. Now let me make sure we both understand. You didn't give her the right kind of converter because you didn't take the time to ask the right questions. Next time, you're going to find out what you need to know—even if you have to drag it out of them."

Jared grinned. "Yep—even if I have to drag it out of them."

(**WHAT IF** Ellie had begun by assuming that Jared had fouled up the data conversion program? How do you think Jared would have responded?)

"That's good," Ray said. "Let me add one point to it. There are really three different reasons why a worker can make a mistake. He:

1. May not know how to do the job correctly,
2. May know, but does it carelessly, or
3. May do it wrong willfully—either intending to do it wrong or not caring whether it's wrong or not.

"When you're correcting a worker, it's important first to find out whether the employee's mistake was willful or careless or the result of not knowing what to do. One of the worst mistakes a manager can make is to treat someone who wasn't sure what to do as though he deliberately did something wrong."

"I certainly agree with that," Ellie replied. "In fact, I find that most errors are made because people don't know what to do. They may never have been told or they may have forgotten, or they haven't taken the time to think it through."

"Right," Ray nodded. "When I find a worker who's made a mistake, I assume that it was an honest mistake. If it was, and I give the person the guidance needed to correct it, I won't see the mistake again.

"On the other hand, if the same mistake pops up again, I start to wonder. Then the individual has to persuade me that it wasn't carelessness or lack of attention or just indifference. In other words, I assume that most conscientious workers won't make the same mistake twice."

Prompt, Automatic Feedback

Bobby Joe Jones, a first-level manager from the next department, comes up just then. "Do you know what I've been trying to do? I've been trying to set up a system so that my workers find out for themselves how they're doing. I figure that if they don't have to get it through me, it can't turn into an argument.

"I've worked something out with the unit that uses our output. If one of my workers produces a document that has an error, the person who uses that document calls the worker directly. My worker either corrects the error over the phone or picks up the document immediately, redoes it, and returns it.

"I had a little trouble persuading both my workgroup and the other unit to adopt this plan, but they finally agreed to test it for 90 days. Our output has improved so much since we started it, though, that I don't think anyone will want to quit using it when the test period is over."

"That's very interesting," Ellie said. "Your people really like it?"

"Most of them do. They know that if they make an error, they'll find out about it quickly. They also know that they won't get blamed for someone else's errors—and that's important. Mike Samuels is the exception; he didn't like it when *I* told him he'd made an error, and he doesn't like it when *someone else* tells him, either. The others think it's great—particularly because I don't even know about an error unless it's repeated. As a matter of fact, the other section doesn't inform me of an error unless it's repeated three times within a two-week period."

"But how do you know how well your people are doing overall?" Ray asked.

"Oh, I still get the biweekly report. It gives me summary figures that tell me how the group is doing as a whole. It's great for making sure we stay within our targets, and I always post it for everyone to see. But I never try to use it to correct individual workers."

The Worker's Responsibility

"What about conduct?" Ray asked. "We've been talking about correcting *performance*, and that's most of what we do. But what about the conduct problems we run into?"

Ellie responded, "I look at conduct almost the same way I do performance. I make sure that everyone knows all the rules, and I try to keep the rules as simple and as few as I can—you know, common sense. After that, each of my people is responsible for his own performance and conduct. I'm not anyone's den mother or schoolteacher, that I should go around taking responsibility for how he behaves."

"I agree," Bobby Joe said. "This Mike Samuels I mentioned before is a good example of a conduct problem. I've talked with him several times, and I've run out of talk. I've made clear what we expect from him and that I won't tolerate anything else. He knows that the next time he's rude to someone in another department, he's in deep trouble. I feel like you do, Ellie—it's his responsibility to improve. The ball's in his court."

EXAMPLE: Dealing with Continued Poor Conduct

Bobby Joe had already talked to Mike several times. Mike knew exactly

What he was doing wrong (being rude to the people who pointed out his errors),

Why it was wrong (he was insulting people who were trying to help him perform well, and refusing to accept useful feedback), and

How to correct it (accept the feedback constructively).

In this final conversation, Bobby Joe gave Mike one last chance to explain himself as they sat together in Bobby Joe's office:

"They keep picking on me. No one else in the unit gets called anywhere near as many times as I do."

"Do you think that's because no one else makes as many errors?"

"It doesn't matter. It's insulting, and I don't like it."

"Okay, Mike, I understand how you feel about it. Now I want to make sure you understand my situation: First of all, our prompt feedback system is policy, and I expect everyone to follow it. Second, rudeness is never acceptable. I don't care what the reason for it is, it simply isn't acceptable.

"Mike, you have a choice. You can clean up your act, do what your job requires, and everything will be fine. If you're not willing to do that, you'd probably better look for another job because I won't tolerate your rudeness another time.

"I've done my part. You know the rules, and you know the consequences if you don't follow them. Mike, we really would like to see you shape up. The people here like you. But we can't make the choice for you. . . ."

(**WHAT IF** the first thing Mike had said was "I've been trying to be nice to those people, but they keep accusing me of making mistakes that I'm not making"? What should Bobby Joe have done then?)

"Let me get in one last thing," Ray said. "We've been emphasizing correcting because it's so important, but correcting alone doesn't motivate people. Showing someone that he did something wrong and then showing him how to do it right won't *motivate* him to do it right. Or don't you agree?"

"I agree," Ellie said. "I've seen managers who think that the way to get workers to produce is to 'get on their case'. Some workers respond to that and won't do good work unless they are yelled at every so often—but they're a small minority."

"Put me down in the 'yes' column, too," Bobby Joe added. "Correcting is necessary, but it's a small part of motivation. I hope there's a good chapter on motivation in this book."

A QUICK SUMMARY

1. Make sure that every worker knows how he's performing. This is the manager's first responsibility where correcting is concerned.

2. Part of being a successful worker is to accept and use correcting, not fight it.

3. A new worker needs to know when he's doing well. Even workers who aren't new should be told occasionally that they're doing well.

4. Whether a worker is new or experienced, make sure he knows right away about any errors he makes. Don't wait.

5. A worker who is making errors needs to know
   a. *What* he isn't doing correctly (or well),
   b. *Why* it isn't right, and
   c. *How* to do it correctly.

6. Showing a worker how to do something right usually means
   a. *Telling* him what to do,
   b. *Showing* him how to do it, and
   c. Letting him *practice* doing it.

7. Sometimes it's not clear whether the worker made an error or not. A good sequence to follow in this situation is:
   a. Always discuss performance (and conduct, too) privately.
   b. Don't assume that you know what happened. Listen to the worker and communicate that you want to listen.
   c. Try to reach an agreement on what happened.
   d. If the worker didn't do anything wrong, make sure he realizes that you know he didn't. End the discussion.
   e. If the worker did make a mistake, give him the chance to realize it.
   f. If you have to point out the mistake, do it as objectively as possible. Don't blame or accuse the worker.
   g. Then make sure the worker understands exactly what he did that was wrong, why it was wrong, and how to do it correctly. If necessary, go through the tell–show–practice sequence.

8. If possible, arrange the work situation so that individual workers find out directly how they are performing. The system should give you overall data, but not data on an individual's performance unless a worker is making repeated errors.

9. It's your responsibility to see that each worker knows the performance and conduct expected of him. It's his responsibility to produce them.

10. As important as correcting is, don't count on it to motivate workers.

StretchMeter 5: CORRECTING

1. I make clear to workers what I expect from them.

NEVER   0   1   2   3   4   5   6   7   8   ALWAYS

2. I get the facts before I decide whether a worker is wrong.

NEVER   0   1   2   3   4   5   6   7   8   ALWAYS

3. I deal with workers' mistakes objectively.

NEVER   0   1   2   3   4   5   6   7   8   ALWAYS

4. I am patient when correcting workers.

NEVER   0   1   2   3   4   5   6   7   8   ALWAYS

5. When I have to correct workers, I do it promptly.

NEVER   0   1   2   3   4   5   6   7   8   ALWAYS

6. I discuss sensitive subjects with workers privately.

NEVER   0   1   2   3   4   5   6   7   8   ALWAYS

7. I try to help workers realize their mistakes for themselves.

NEVER   0   1   2   3   4   5   6   7   8   ALWAYS

Correcting ASAP

1. Effective correcting begins with being clear—or it doesn't begin at all. If you're reading this at work, put the book down, go to a worker, and check to see that he knows exactly how to do the most important part of his job. Over the next week, check with each worker at least once on some important aspect of the job. (If you're not reading this at work, do it as soon as you arrive.)

2. Before you decide whether a worker made a mistake or not, you have to get the facts. Make up your mind right now that you'll never tell a worker that he made a mistake until you're certain that's what happened. (Most of the time, you can't be certain until you've heard the worker's side of it.) To help you remember this in the situation, use a Reaction Alert (see the ASAP in Chapter 1 for details).

3. Perhaps you believe that workers make mistakes on purpose. Even if this belief is unconscious, it's harmful. To see the difference an objective attitude makes, tell yourself that for the next 30 days, you're *not* going to get "angry" or "disappointed" when someone makes a mistake. (If you need to, use a Reaction Alert—see ASAP 2.)

4. Some workers require a great deal of correcting before they begin to recognize their mistakes and take responsibility for them. It may help you to remember that correcting your workers is a key part of your job—not just something you're forced to do until you can get back to more important work. (ASAP 3 in Chapter 1 may be useful to you.)

5. Nothing is as easy, or as dangerous, as postponing correcting your workers. You just have to decide you're going to correct them, and then do it. Starting tomorrow morning, when a worker does something less than well, discuss it with him *immediately*. Do it for one week. Then another. Then another. . . .

6. Correcting workers in private, shows them they have your respect. Unlike some changes, this one doesn't take much effort. Just *do* it.

7. Each of us would rather find our mistakes and correct them than have someone else point them out to us. Making a change here can take

some practice. Write yourself a note that says that when you have a performance discussion with a worker, you'll give him the opportunity to discover the mistake for himself. Then follow through. You may have some problems at first, and it won't work all of the time, but keep trying. It pays handsome dividends.

CHAPTER 8

Motivating

PHASE ONE MANAGEMENT	C
Structuring	O
Selecting	M
Guiding	M
Correcting	U
Motivating	N
Delegating	I
Supporting	C
	A
	T
	I
	N
	G

In this chapter, you'll find useful information on:

The importance of creating a work environment that motivates workers.

How to deal with workers who are motivated by different aspects of the job.

How to recognize critical motivators that are almost completely under the manager's control.

Would you be surprised to know that this chapter will help you develop workers who are motivated to do well? I didn't think you would.

WHAT IS EFFECTIVE MOTIVATING?

Interviewer: Ms. Martinez, we certainly appreciate your giving us this interview today.

Ms. Martinez: You're more than welcome.

Interviewer: Let me come right to the point. As you see it, what do we mean when we say a worker is motivated?

Ms. Martinez: A motivated worker is one who does willingly what the organization wants him to do.

Interviewer: That's interesting. And how do you motivate workers? Pep talks, motivational programs, free trips, threats, motivational courses, or what?

Ms. Martinez: Well, I don't use any of those. I try to set my workgroup up so that the best way for my workers to get what they want is to do what the organization wants them to do.

Interviewer: That's very interesting. But you must do some other things to motivate them. . . .

Ms. Martinez: No. Workers can only be motivated by themselves, not by me. I try to see that

1. They get rewarded for doing good work, and rewarded even more for doing great work;
2. They never get rewarded for doing a so-so job; and
3. They never get penalized for doing their best.

They do the rest.

Interviewer: That's part of it, but I'm sure there's more. Maybe you use motivational tapes, or sing company songs as do the Japanese, or . . .

Ms. Martinez: No, that's really all. And now, if you'll excuse me, I have work to do.

Interviewer: But. . . .

WHY IS EFFECTIVE MOTIVATING IMPORTANT?

Why was Anita Martinez so firm about not trying to motivate her workers?

First of all, she'd learned from experience that trying to "motivate" workers with pep talks, slogans, tapes, and all the rest brings only short-term success, at best. Sometimes these methods can recharge a work-group or pull it through a bad time, but they never work over the long haul. These are all "external motivators"; reliable motivation comes from within.

Besides, when Anita put a lot of time and energy into trying to *motivate* her workgroup, she found she didn't have time to manage it. She got frustrated in a hurry, and this didn't do much for *her* motivation.

Anita was in a quandary, though. She knew that her workers needed to be motivated or they wouldn't get their work done. But if she spent all her time trying to motivate them, *her* job wouldn't get done. What was the solution?

At that point, Anita made a good decision. She talked with two of her best workers to get some feedback from their side. She found that the people in her group resented the motivational materials even more than she did. To her workers, the materials were insulting because they seemed to suggest that the workers wouldn't do a good job on their own. Anita discovered that her people *already* wanted to do a good job, but each for a different reason: job satisfaction, advancement, better pay, being part of a successful team, not letting her down, or something else entirely. The common thread of motivation was the work itself and the work environment.

That's when Anita got the message and changed her approach. Instead of "motivating" her workers, she used her time to see that their jobs brought out the best in them. As she spent less and less time on mo-tivating, the workgroup performed better and better.

HOW DO I MOTIVATE EFFECTIVELY?

Anita Martinez: Look, I really need your help. You're my two best workers, and you're two of my best-motivated workers. I've tried and tried, but I just don't know how to motivate some of these people.

Tony Amico: You're a nice person and I like working for you, so I'm going to tell you the truth. We all wish you'd cut out the "motivational" stuff. I've heard those pitches dozens of times. As far as I'm con-cerned, they just take time away from doing the job.

Ernie Washington: Yeah, me too. If you had to depend on that cr . . . uh, stuff to get me to work, we'd all be up the creek.

Anita: Okay, I hear you loud and clear. But what do I do instead?

Ernie: For openers, you could forget all this rubbish about *you* having to motivate *us.* Pep talks might help keep us going in tough times, but that's about it. People get motivated by what happens to them on the job day after day—and that means you can be motivated not to do the job just as easily as you can be motivated to do it.

Anita: I'm not sure what you mean.

Reverse Motivation

Tony: I know what he means. When I first started here, over in receiving, I really wanted to do a good job. It wasn't hard for me to log in 25 percent more shipments than the standard. I did this for a few days, though, and the senior worker—a guy named Charlie—had a little talk with me. He explained that what I was doing made the others look bad and that I should quit being a "rate-buster." I didn't like what he said, but the supervisor didn't seem to care, and the extra effort wasn't making me any more money. So, I slacked off—and I got along fine with the rest of the group from then on out.

Ernie: Yeah, I was in a group like that. We got a new supervisor, and he tried using this motivation stuff on us, too. Nothing happened. There just wasn't any reason for anybody to do more than we were already doing.

Anita: You mean that if you aren't paid for the extra work, you won't do it?

Tony: Nah, it's not that simple. The point is that Ernie and me and all the rest are going to do what pays off for us. On those jobs we were talking about, it paid off to do what the others were doing. So that's what we did.

Ernie: Yeah—look at it this way. In those groups, people weren't producing their best for three reasons:

1. There wasn't any payoff for doing your best. As long as you logged in enough work to meet the standard, you got the same paycheck.

2. You actually got punished for doing your best. The way the group was set up, anybody who worked hard made everybody else mad. And the supervisor made it worse because he was always saying he didn't want any conflict.

3. You were rewarded for not doing your best. It kept you in good with the group, and it made the supervisor happy.

That supervisor was doing a tremendous job of motivating all of us— to do a so-so job. I left as soon as I could.

EXAMPLE: Reverse Motivation

"Tony, can I talk with you for a minute?"

"Sure, Charlie—what's up?"

"Tony, I know you want to do a good job, and we appreciate that. But you're going to get us all in trouble. You don't want to do that, do you?"

"No—but I don't know what you're talking about."

"You've been putting away too much material. What have you done the last couple of weeks—20 percent over standard?"

"About that, I guess. It isn't very hard to do."

"It may not be hard, but it's dangerous. Don't you realize that if everyone started working at your rate, management would make it the new rate. Then we'd all have to work that much harder just to get the same paycheck. You don't want that, do you?" He clapped Tony on the shoulder.

"No, no I don't. But it seems to me that we ought to do as good a job as we can."

"My boy, you're just naive. What management wants is to get as much work out of us for as little money as possible. We're giving them what they're paying us for now—and the boys would be awfully upset if you screwed that up for everybody. . . ."

(**WHAT IF** Tony had kept on producing over standard? What do you think would have happened then?)

Anita: It still sounds to me like you're saying you should get more money if you do more than the standard. And don't get me wrong—I agree.

Limiting Motivation

Tony: Sometimes that's true, and sometimes it isn't. My last job was straight piecework. You produced 80 percent of the standard, or they fired you. If you turned out 110 percent or more, you got a bonus—depending on how much you produced.

Anita: That sounds pretty good.

Tony: It was, in a way. We did produce more. But the morale there was bad. People wouldn't work together. They were all working on their own rates, and to hell with anybody else.

You see, they didn't pay for anything except the number of pieces each person turned out that day. It didn't do you any good to help somebody else or try to help things in general. Most of us had ideas about how to do the work better, but we never told them to anyone. We figured that as soon as we did, management would put the idea into use, give the guy who came up with it a pat on the back, and raise the rate on us.

Different Strokes . . .

Anita: Okay, pep talks don't work, and extra pay for producing above standard doesn't always work. What does?

Ernie: The problem is that different people work for different reasons. Me and Tony, we really like being inspectors because it's an interesting job. We learn about a bunch of different products, and our work takes us through most of the warehouse. You'd have to pay us a lot more money to get us to take a job that wasn't this interesting. But if the job got boring, we'd leave.

Now Tomas, he's in it strictly for the money. He took the job to get the 35-cent-an-hour raise that came with it. He'll produce what he gets paid to produce, and he'll transfer out just as soon as he finds a job that pays better.

Tony: Here's another example. Mary and Reid don't care much about either the work or the money. Oh, they'd both move on if the pay got really bad or the work got too demanding. The reason they're here, though, is that they like the work environment. They like the people, and they like the fact that you're not hassling them all the time. They're going to give you whatever the group thinks is a fair day's work, so they don't cause any trouble.

Ernie: Let me give you two more quick examples. You've been having trouble with Arnold lately, haven't you? You know why? Arnold thinks you ought to answer a lot more questions for him. Bernice, though, would be out of here in a minute if you started butting in on her job. She wants to do it her way, and as long as she's getting it done she doesn't want *anyone* hassling her.

Anita: Wow! As well as I know all of you, I never realized all this. If I hear you right, you're saying that

1. You and Tony are motivated because you like the work;
2. Tomas is motivated because we pay him well, and he doesn't really care about the work;
3. Mary and Reid work here, not because of either the work or the money, but because they like the work environment;
4. Arnold isn't as motivated as he could be because he wants to lean on me more; and
5. Bernice only produces well if she's left alone to do everything her own way.

Tony: That's about the size of it.

EXAMPLE: Different Motivators

If you were to ask some of Anita's workers why they liked being in that unit, this is what they might say:

"It pays well," Tomas says. "I want to get a bass boat, and with this job I can afford it. My wife and I can afford to go out to eat at a good restaurant once a month."

"I really like the people here," Mary says. "We all get along very well, and it's a nice place to work. It's not tense, and the people aren't at each other's throats like they were at my last job."

"Well, I guess it's okay," Arnold says. "I think that Ms. Martinez ought to give us more guidance and help us more. I really don't think she takes her job as seriously as she should."

"This is the best job I've ever had," says Bernice. "Everybody stays out of my hair and lets me do my job. If there's anything I can't stand, it's a boss who keeps looking over your shoulder—and Ms. Martinez never does that. She's okay."

(**WHAT IF** Ms. Martinez began supervising everyone closely? How would Arnold and Bernice's reactions change?)

Anita: It sounds like an impossible job—trying to motivate such different people!

Ernie: As a matter of fact, you're doing pretty well. Everybody except Arnold is doing a good job. Look at what we've got:

1. Most of the people think the work is interesting even if they don't get as excited about it as Tony and me.

2. The pay is good. You do a good job of seeing that we get our bonuses when we earn them. Even if the rest of us don't work for money in the same way Tomas does, getting our bonuses on time makes us think that the organization appreciates our effort.

3. This is a good place to work. You've made some changes that make it more pleasant, we all get along well, and you're better to work for than a lot of managers. I've even heard Tomas and Bernice say they like being part of the group.

4. And you let us alone to do our work. I'd talk a lot more about that, except I have a feeling that the next chapter's going to get into that subject.

Anita: But what about Arnold? And I think Sandy feels the same way—what about him?

Tony: I'll tell you what I'd do. Mr. Purcell in shipping has a group of inspectors just about like us. And he's always telling his people what to do. I have two good friends over there who'd love to move over here. You could talk to Arnold and Sandy. If they really do want somebody to tell them what to do more often, maybe you and Mr. Purcell could do some switching. I remember reading not long ago that one of the rules for picking workers was that they should be comfortable in the workgroup—maybe a switch would make every-one happier.

Anita: Hey, you guys have been very helpful! Thank you.

Some Rules for Effective Motivating

Some time later, Anita told Frederick Holst, a good friend and manager of the purchasing agents, about her discussion with Tony and Ernie.

"That was good," Fred said, "but I'd like to add my five rules for motivating:

Rule 1: Always notice a job well done. You don't have to do anything elaborate: a pat on the back, a quick note, whatever. The important thing is letting the worker know that you're aware of and appreciate what he did.

And notice that I said 'a job well done.' With a new worker, you want to give him an 'attaboy' even if he does just part of the job right. That's a job well done, for a new worker. It's either Mr. Johnson or Mr. Blanchard down the hall that has a great way of putting it: Catch a worker doing something right, and let him know you caught him.

It's pretty much the same with an experienced worker who's been slipping. You want to notice any improvement (which is, by definition, a job well done), and you want him to know that you've noticed. Sometimes it's more difficult to learn to do good work again than to learn it in the first place.

And, for heaven's sake, don't overlook the worker who *always* does well. Never take your good people for granted. They need to know you appreciate their continually good performance.

EXAMPLE: Noticing a Job Well Done

"Edna, that's the fourth report you've typed without an error. Fantastic!"

"Molly, I just checked your drawings, and they're excellent. At the rate you're picking things up, you won't be a trainee much longer."

"Kareem, you've driven for two years without an accident. I've asked everybody to come in half an hour early on Friday so they can see you get your safety award."

"Paul, your sales for the month still aren't as good as they should be. That was the bad news. The good news is that you've improved 37 percent in the last three months. At this rate, you'll be back on target by the end of May. I think that's great—and I really appreciate the effort you're putting into this.

"I want to start our meeting by announcing that Mona's PC program for small purchases is going to be used in all 17 regions. She's done us all proud!"

(**WHAT IF** the manager hadn't noticed the job well done in each case? What difference would it make?)

Rule 2 goes along with Rule 1: *Always recognize people as quickly as you can after they've done a job well.* Do it right on the spot if you can. If not, do it as soon as possible. Our recognition program doesn't always help much—it usually takes anywhere from a week to three months to get a formal award through the system. I use it, but it's strictly secondary.

When someone does something well, he feels good about it. When you notice him right away, it makes him feel even better. If you wait a week or a month, it's old news. By then, he probably won't have any feelings about it anymore—except maybe to be irritated that it took you so long to notice.

EXAMPLE: Quick Recognition

"Charlene, I saw how you helped Maurice with his packing just then. Teamwork like that is what keeps us on top—thanks!"

"I called you all together to tell you that an hour ago Beyta caught a purse-snatcher and held him until the police arrived. Beyta, I can promise you that you'll get an award for this—but I wanted everybody to know right away what a tremendous thing you did."

"Sam, I saw how hard you were working to make sure you had that connection right. Thanks—I really appreciate the extra effort."

(**WHAT IF** you were one of these workers? How would you feel about what the manager said?)

Rule 3 is a sort of reverse recognition: *People who aren't performing well should always be a little uncomfortable.* If a person is trying, recognize all of his improvements—but make sure he keeps the goal in mind. If he's *not* trying, push him to make a career decision. I don't mean harass him. But you might want to help him get a transfer or another job if he's not happy working for you. Whatever you do, never assure him that 'it's alright' not to perform well.

EXAMPLE: Keeping Poor Performers Uncomfortable

"Fred, I understand that you feel a lot of pressure to increase your output. Frankly, I think you ought to. It's important that everyone carry his share of the load."

"Yan, I realize the others aren't being very kind to you right now. In a way, I'm sorry. But they feel they're having to do most of your work, and I don't really blame them for being angry. I think if you show them you can do a first-rate job, though, you'll find things will change in a hurry."

"Marty, that's simply not acceptable work. I expect you to stay and redo it until it is."

(**WHAT IF** each of these workers feels comfortable with his level of performance? What happens to his performance?)

Rule 4 is the one we all tend to forget: *The recognition that one worker gets from another is very important.* I have a Gold Star program. When a worker does something that helps another get his job done, the person he helped gives him a Gold Star. Three Gold Stars let a worker go home two hours early on Friday afternoon. I really think, though, that for most of my people, just the good feeling from the Gold Star is enough.

It doesn't matter what you use or how it happens. The important thing is to create a workgroup where the workers *want* to give each other recognition and know that you encourage it.

EXAMPLE: Workers Recognizing One Another

"Sarah, the way you've helped Charlie and me the last few days has been tremendous. I'm going to tell Mr. Jones that you should be Employee of the Month for sure this time."

"Ms. Peters, I just want everybody here to know that if it hadn't been for Wynona and Carlos's help on the Foster project, I never would have finished on time. They were really great."

"Mort, you've earned your wings this week. Mary Lou, Willie, and Laurie have all made a point of telling me how helpful you've been to them. I just want you to know I appreciate it, too."

(**WHAT IF** a manager keeps making note of the recognition workers give one another? What is likely to happen to their recognition of each other?)

Rule 5 can be used to support every one of the first four rules: *Always work with your workgroup and the individuals in it to help them set improvement goals.* It's much easier for people to improve their performance—individually and together—if they have specific goals.

Goals are funny things. When people set goals, the goals themselves become motivators. You can almost say that a good goal *pulls* good performance out of people. And when someone achieves a goal, that's a logical place to recognize what he's done.

EXAMPLE: Encouraging Improvement Goals

"I've passed out pocket-sized cards to all of you. Page two has the division goals on it, and page three has our branch goals. I want each of you to put your two or three most important personal goals on page four. I'll drop by and talk with you one-on-one Monday and Tuesday to see what you've got. We've discussed them before, but if you need any help before then, come see me."

"Red, I know how hard it is to get back in gear when no one's pushed you for good performance in a long time. I know you can do it—that's why I persuaded Mr. Emmert to keep you on. But you need to set some clear performance goals for yourself. I don't expect you to do everything at once—but I want you to draft some realistic monthly goals and discuss them with me at nine o'clock, Friday morning."

"Bernadette, you're the most consistent producer I have. Would you be willing to work with me on a couple of goals for this coming year? I'd like to see you develop your presentation skills so that you could give the monthly update instead of me."

(**WHAT IF** Bernadette didn't want to work on presentation skills?)

"What's most important about all the rules is that they're things *you can control*. They don't depend on the organization's recognition program or pay system or anything else. *And* they're all things that matter to workers."

"I sure do thank you." Anita said, "Before I forget all these things, I'd better make myself . . ."

A QUICK SUMMARY

1. Managers don't have time to do their other jobs and keep "motivating" workers, too.

2. In fact, workers can only motivate themselves. They will only do what they believe pays off for them. If they think that doing above-average work will get them into trouble, they will be motivated to do mediocre work.

3. It's the manager's job to create a work situation where doing what the organization needs is what pays off for workers. This means that workers:

    a. Get rewarded for doing good work and rewarded even more for doing great work,

    b. Never get rewarded for doing a so-so job, and

    c. Never get penalized for doing their best.

4. Different people are motivated in different ways. Here are some of the most common motivators:

    a. The work itself,

    b. The pay,

    c. A pleasant work environment,

    d. A pleasant and helpful manager, and

    e. The freedom to do the job one's own way.

5. A good manager tries to know the main motivators of each of his people, and to create a workgroup that is motivating in as many ways as possible.

6. Although a manager can't always control everything that motivates his people, he can control some very critical motivators by:

   a. Always recognizing a job well done;

   b. Always recognizing people as quickly as possible after they've done well;

   c. Always relating whatever is being recognized to good performance;

   d. Never letting workers who aren't performing well be comfortable with their performance;

   e. Encouraging workers to recognize each other for cooperation and teamwork; and

   f. Encouraging workers, and working with them to set improvement goals constantly.

StretchMeter 6: MOTIVATING

1. I try to create a work situation that motivates my workers.

NEVER   0   1   2   3   4   5   6   7   8   ALWAYS

2. My workers are rewarded only if they do a good job.

NEVER   0   1   2   3   4   5   6   7   8   ALWAYS

3. My workers are encouraged to do their best without penalty.

NEVER   0   1   2   3   4   5   6   7   8   ALWAYS

4. I understand what motivates each of my workers.

NEVER   0   1   2   3   4   5   6   7   8   ALWAYS

5. I recognize a job well done.

NEVER   0   1   2   3   4   5   6   7   8   ALWAYS

6. I recognize workers quickly for what they do.

NEVER   0   1   2   3   4   5   6   7   8   ALWAYS

7. I relate all recognition to good performance.

NEVER   0   1   2   3   4   5   6   7   8   ALWAYS

8. I see to it that poor performers are uncomfortable.

NEVER   0   1   2   3   4   5   6   7   8   ALWAYS

9. I encourage workers to recognize each other.

NEVER   0   1   2   3   4   5   6   7   8   ALWAYS

10. I encourage workers to set improvement goals.

NEVER   0   1   2   3   4   5   6   7   8   ALWAYS

Motivating ASAP

1. If the work situation doesn't motivate your workers, they probably won't be motivated. Look at the five different kinds of motivation that Anita, Tony, and Ernie were discussing. Which one of them can you influence most quickly? Within the next week, make at least one change that will make this more of a motivator. Keep making changes, with this motivator and the others. Don't ever stop.

2. Workers have been rewarded even if they didn't do a good job? Starting now, begin to change this. If you're rewarding them for less than good performance, stop it! If your boss is rewarding them for less than good performance, get him to stop it! Whatever you have to do, stop it!

3. If workers are penalized for doing their best, stop it! All of the comments in ASAP 2 apply.

4. If you truly understand motivation, you understand that each of your workers is motivated individually. Get a small memo pad or notebook and label a page for each worker. For the next week, listen carefully, ask discreet questions, and identify *at least* one motivator for each worker. Use that as basic training. Keep identifying motivators from now on.

5. Do you still believe that workers ought to do good work without any recognition? No one (including yourself?) wants to be taken for granted. For the next week, make a point of identifying and recognizing *at least* one instance of good performance each day. Try to recognize good performance with each worker at least once during the period. Then keep at it—until you retire.

6. It's easy to put off recognizing workers. In fact, the recognition programs of many organizations encourage such procrastination because they take so long. For the next week, recognize at least one worker each day immediately for a job well done.[1] Then keep doing it.

[1] Perhaps I'd better insert a warning here. Don't be phoney in your recognition! If you can't find something you can genuinely recognize, don't recognize anything. If you can't honestly praise a person, don't praise him. (If you honestly can't find anyone or anything to praise in your workgroup—you are in serious, serious trouble. Either you need to change workgroups or they badly need to change you.)

7. Remember, the name of the game is production. Make a note: the next time you're going to recognize someone for something other than performance, you're going to relate it to performance. You can't? Then you should ask yourself whether this is really something you want to recognize.

8. You should cultivate a genuine empathy with your workgroup—but don't feel sorry for nonperformers. If you have any nonperformers and they aren't uncomfortable, it's time to change that. Don't pick on them, or embarrass them, or freeze them out. Just make sure they're not quite happy with their performance. Start now.[2]

9. If your workgroup is successful, your workers ought to be recognizing each other constantly. If they're not, you need to intervene. Ask: Are they helping each other? If they're not, you have work to do to make the group fully successful (see Chapter 12 for more information on that). If they are, you need to notice and encourage the times when they recognize the help they give each other.

10. Improvement goals are amongst the great motivators. Sit down tomorrow morning and sketch out a plan to help your people develop some. The plan should include: (1) making clear to your workers what improvement goals are and why you want them, (2) helping them set realistic goals and timetables, and (3) discussing their progress with them. Then implement the plan. (A word of caution: Don't approach this plan as something to be forced on your workers, but as an opportunity for them to become even more successful.)

---

[2]Perhaps a word of caution is needed here, too. Many workgroups have individuals who aren't world-beaters but who take care of the jobs that someone has to do. If you have someone who can't produce like the others, but who does these jobs well, he may not be a nonperformer. The key is whether your best workers see him as "getting by" without having to produce. If the answer is "yes," you have a nonperformer.

CHAPTER 9

Delegating

PHASE ONE MANAGEMENT	
Structuring	C
Selecting	O
Guiding	M
Correcting	M
	U
Motivating	N
Delegating	I
Supporting	C
	A
	T
	I
	N
	G

In this chapter, you'll find useful information on:

The three basic principles of delegating.

The rules for successful delegating— including the five levels of delegation.

How to let workers solve their own problems.

Delegating encourages workers to take responsibility for their jobs. *It also helps* motivate them to do well. *When you delegate fully, you find out if your* workers know *what to do, how to do it well,* and *when they've done it well.*

WHAT IS EFFECTIVE DELEGATING?

K ay Ishikawa has strong opinions about effective delegating:

"Effective delegating is a way of harnessing the energy of your people that can't be matched.

"Some managers think that workers are there simply to do the jobs they're hired to do and follow directions. In my experience, workers are too well educated and self-aware to accept this kind of treatment. It doesn't recognize the hidden abilities workers have, and it treats them as though they were machines.

"A really effective manager educates his workers by passing along his knowledge and experience to them by guiding them on the job. Just to make them smarter? No. His real goal is to produce self-sufficient workers. When the workers have reached that state, and they know the manager's basic policy, the manager can then simply delegate authority to them and let them handle the job.

"Will the workers make mistakes? Of course. The mistakes they make, though, are a small price to pay for the growth you can expect in your workgroup. Delegating allows workers to make full use of their abilities. People aren't like machines; they like to use their heads. Delegating unlocks your workers' unlimited potential.

"But you need to remember that effective delegating requires clear thinking. You delegate only what you can *effectively* delegate. If the worker is fully successful, you let him do the job without interference from you. If he isn't completely successful, you don't delegate quite so much. But you always delegate, and you always push your workgroup toward being more responsible, having more authority.

"If you do it carefully and thoughtfully, if you build up your workers' trust in you and let them use their abilities, they'll produce first-class work for you willingly."

WHY IS SUCCESSFUL DELEGATING IMPORTANT?

Earline Walton knows:

"When I put myself into the shoes of the people who are working for me, I know that the more freedom I'm given, the more opportunity to be creative I'm given, the more I'm going to enjoy my job and want to come to work. And I'll do a better job when I'm there.

"I didn't use to manage that way. I'd hang over people's shoulders to see that they were doing everything just right. Then I realized all the attention and effort I was giving them was teaching them to be dependent on me rather than to rely on themselves. That was a valuable piece of information for me. Now I make whatever I need very clear, and I make it clear that they can do it. In other words, I let them be successful.

"Besides, I don't have time to do their jobs or their thinking for them. If I let myself get tied down that way, I wouldn't have time to do what really matters to me. I would keep them from being successful, and I'd keep myself from being successful, too. No thanks!"[1]

HOW DO I DELEGATE EFFECTIVELY?

"Amelia, this idea of delegating really makes me nervous."

"Why, Bill? Delegating can be tricky, but you don't need to be scared of it."

"Mr. Jankowski was just talking with me about delegating. He said I should delegate everything I can to my workers. I'd like to do that, but I'm afraid of what might happen. I know my people too well. They just couldn't handle it."

[1]Although the other speakers in this book are not based on specific individuals (their names are made up, and they're composites of many people I've known), that's not the case with Kay and Earline.

The words of "Kay Ishikawa" are based on those of Kaoru Ishikawa, one of the foremost Japanese experts on quality control. Much of what Kay says is paraphrased from Mr. Ishikawa's book *What Is Total Quality Control? The Japanese Way*, translated by David J. Lu (Englewood Cliffs, N.J.: Prentice-Hall, 1985).

"Earline Walton" is a fictitious name, but much of what she says is paraphrased from an interview in Jim Wall's book, *Bosses* (Lexington, Mass.: Lexington Books, 1987). The person being interviewed is the manager of a bordello.

I thought that if you knew that two people as different as this believe so strongly in delegation, you'd take it seriously, too!

"Couldn't handle it? Why?"

"They're just not ready for it. They don't know the jobs well enough yet."

The Basic Principles of Delegating

"Bill, if you want to be successful at delegating, you have to keep three principles in mind:

1. Your primary goal is to delegate to your workers responsibility and authority for their work. You've got to be clear about this, and you've got to communicate it clearly to your workers. Until you've done so, they won't be successful workers and you won't be a successful manager. In fact, you can almost say that the reason you do structuring, selecting, guiding, correcting, and motivating is so that you can delegate successfully. It's that important.

2. You always delegate what people are ready to handle—keeping in mind that you want to keep stretching them a little. There's something of a knack in knowing just how much to delegate when, but you'll pick that up.

3. You need to keep tabs on your delegations. When you have a completely successful worker who takes full responsibility for his job, you can delegate and not worry about it. Anything less than that, though, and you need to make sure that the delegation gets completed—and completed right."

EXAMPLE: How *Not* to Delegate

"Broderick, we're glad to have you with us. You need to understand right off that I know this business better than anyone else, and I make the decisions around here. If you're good at listening and doing what you're told, you'll get along fine."

"Gosh, Mr. Abel, I have a couple of ideas about how we might . . ."

"Not necessary—just follow instructions and everything will be fine."

"Frampton, I know you've only been with us a short time, but I need someone to take this project and run with it. Here's a brief sketch of what needs to be done. You take care of it for me, okay?"

"Gosh, Ms. Baxter, I don't really understand what some of this is about. . . ."

"You'll do fine. I know you'll figure it out. Now go handle it, and let me get on with my work."

"Darn it, Celecia, I was really counting on you to have this done. I know that today is the date I mentioned to you."

"I remember clearly, Mr. Cleve, that you said that you'd like for me to *try* to get it done by today. I did try, I really did."

"I should have known—if you want something done right around here, you have to do it yourself! Give it to me, and I'll take care of it."

(**WHAT IF** you were the boss of Mr. Abel, Ms. Baxter, or Mr. Cleve? What would you say to them?)

"Your three principles of delegation sound good, Amelia, but I'm not sure just how to apply them."

The Rules of Delegating

"Believe it or not, Bill, it isn't that hard—if you set your delegations up right and follow through on them. I was reading a manual for new managers the other day that offered a good set of rules for delegation. Are you interested?"

"Of course."

"Okay, here they are—

Rule 1: When you delegate, be very clear about what you're delegating. It might help you to think about the five levels of delegation:

a. *Complete delegation:* Use this with a fully successful worker. You tell him what you want done, give him the due date, and then leave it up to him. The only thing he owes you is to tell you when he completes it.

b. *Substantial delegation:* Use this with a good but not completely successful worker. You tell him what you want done and when the deadline is, but this time, he reports back to you *before* the work is finalized. The worker has a great deal of freedom, but you also get the chance to discuss what's going to be done before it actually takes place. This level of delegation has two time targets: (1) the date by which the worker will report to you on his plans for the project, and (2) the date by which the project will be completed.

By the way, when you make a substantial delegation, it means that you intend for the worker to make the necessary decision. You allow yourself a final chance to look at the decision, but both you and the worker should assume that the decision is still his. If you have reservations about the worker's decision, discuss it with him—in hopes that one of you will persuade the other. Don't overrule the worker's decision unless it's absolutely necessary. If you intend to make the decision yourself, start out with a limited delegation, not a substantial one.

c. *Limited delegation:* Use this with a worker who is good but even less successful. You tell him what needs to be done, and he gets back to you with recommendations. You're going to make the final decision. In this case, the time target isn't when he will complete the delegation, but when he will give you the recommendations. Then you set the final target, depending on the recommendation you choose.

d. *Minimal delegation:* Use this with a new worker or a poor worker who's improving. Never accept this level of delegation for a worker as a continuing situation. At this level, you assign the job *and* tell the worker how to do it and when to do it. His only responsibility is to do what you tell him on schedule. In this case, you may also set up some dates by when you want progress reports from him.

e. *No delegation:* Avoid this whenever you can. This is the level where you tell the worker that you'll decide whether you want something done, and if you do, you'll get back to him. That leaves the ball in your court and takes any initiative away from the worker. In this case, there aren't any time targets at all."[2]

---

[2]I've borrowed heavily here from William Oncken's book, *Managing Management Time* (Englewood Cliffs, N.J.: Prentice-Hall, 1984). It's a super book, and it's mentioned in "Your Own Management University" at the end of this book.

EXAMPLE: Levels of Delegation

"Meyer, Marketing needs a new projected sales report. Hanna Jenks in the Analysis Branch knows what they need. Get together with her and set it up for them. Let me know when you're finished." **(complete delegation)**

"Meyer, Marketing needs a new projected sales report. Go talk to Hanna Jenks in the Analysis Branch and find out what they need. Work out your design, and get on my calendar to go over it with me next Friday. As soon as you talk with Ms. Jenks, let me know if you think it'll affect any of your other priorities."* **(substantial delegation)**

"Meyer, Marketing needs a new projected sales report. See Hanna Jenks in the Analysis Branch and find out what they need. Figure out three or four different ways we could get the information for them, and get back to me next Friday." **(limited delegation)**

"Meyer, Marketing needs a new projected sales report. I want you to talk with Hanna Jenks in the Analysis Branch. Find out exactly what she wants: the purpose of it, how much detail, how often—the works. Get the information to me by Thursday. After I've had a chance to look at it, I'll let you know what I want you to do." **(minimal delegation)**

"Meyer, I understand that Marketing wants a new projected sales report. I may need you to do something with it, and I'll let you know if I do." **(no delegation)**

(**WHAT IF** you were Meyer? How would you feel about each delegation?)

*Notice that at the complete level the manager didn't mention priorities. That's because he expects Meyer to identify any conflicts in priorities and see that they get resolved. (This can happen either because Meyer resolves them or, if appropriate, lets the manager resolve them.) Below that level, the manager makes sure that conflicting priorities get resolved.

"I want to ask you some more about Rule 1, Amelia, but I think I understand the basics. What's next?"

"*Rule 2: Be sure every delegation has a specific time target.* This may be the date by which it's to be done, or the date by which you want a progress report or recommendation. But never let a worker walk out of your office with an assignment that doesn't have a clear time target. In fact, for everything except complete delegation or no delegation, you should set a specific day and time for getting back together with the worker.

EXAMPLE: Setting Specific Time Targets

"Tvet, this special order needs to be out of here by ten o'clock tomorrow morning."

"Barney, find a way to schedule this job in so that it can be done by April 17. Have Ada put you on my calendar for three o'clock tomorrow afternoon so you can tell me how you intend to do it."

"Henrietta, you know all about Acme's requirements for its new computer system. I want you to draw up at least three alternative configurations for me to review. See that Mike puts you on my calendar no later than next Wednesday morning. You can give me the alternatives, and then I'll make a decision."

"Muncie, these are the changes that have to be made in the Pioneer estimate. Have the revised estimate in final form to me by three o'clock this afternoon."

(**WHAT IF** you had to delegate a project to Sandra, a new worker? What level(s) of delegation would you consider?)

Rule 3: Make it clear that time targets are to be met. It is *not* acceptable for a worker to walk in the day something is due to tell you it won't be done on time. All workers are capable of thinking ahead and keeping track of dates. Whenever a worker sees that a target time is going to be missed, he should get with you at least several days in advance to discuss the situation. Anything else is completely unsatisfactory.

EXAMPLE: Seeing That Time Targets Are Met

"Wesley, it really breaks my heart to have to mark your project 'Unsatisfactory.'"

"That can't be right, Mr. Bergman. I gave you everything you asked me for."

"You did indeed—but you gave it to me a day late."

"For heaven's sake! It was just one day, and I had other things I had to do too."

"That doesn't matter. The rules we run by are perfectly clear. You had an assigned project, and you were late; which automatically makes it unsatisfactory work, and that's how it's going down on the books. If everything you do for the next month is on time, I'll consider upgrading it. Miss one more deadline without working it out with me beforehand, and this stays 'Unsatisfactory' forever."

(**WHAT IF** Mr. Bergman said "It's really 'Unsatisfactory,' but I'll overlook it this time"? What would that communicate to Wesley?)

Rule 4: It's never your responsibility to follow up to 'see how he's doing.' This is the clearest symptom of poor delegation; it's really a form of 'pestering.' In the first place, it keeps the worker from being responsible for the delegation. Good workers will resent the follow-up, while poor workers will depend on it. Also, if you feel you need to follow up, it probably means you're not comfortable with the degree of delegation you made—or that you neglected to set realistic time targets. Any way you look at it, it's a mistake.

EXAMPLE: The Consequences of "Following Up"

"Emily, I thought your project was due today."

"Oh my goodness, Mr. Dvorak, it is, isn't it? Why didn't you remind me of it sooner?"

"I shouldn't have to remind you of . . . oh, Tom, how are you coming with the internal review summary?"

"Glad you asked. I've been working on something else, and the summary just slipped my mind. I'll get right on it."

"Please see that you do, Tom—it's important to get things done on time, you know. Now, Emily, back to your project. When do you expect to have it done?"

"Well, I can work on it tomorrow afternoon. . . ."

"Excuse me a moment, Emily. Rifaat, how's the quarterly projection coming?"

"I haven't started it yet, Mr. Dvorak. Remind me of it again on Tuesday, will you?"

"I'll see if I can remember, but you really ought to . . . oh, never mind. Now, Emily, back to you."

"Excuse me, Mr. Dvorak, but I have to get some papers together that I promised Mrs. Hurst I'd deliver to her yesterday. Could you please catch me later this afternoon?"

"But I . . . but . . . but. . . ."

(**WHAT IF** Mr. Dvorak started insisting that everyone meet his own deadlines without "follow-ups from him?" How do you think his workers would react initially?)

Rule 5: You and the worker share the responsibility for understanding what's to be done. You should be specific, and you should check to see that he understands just what you want done. But the worker must take responsibility for understanding, and ask you for more information when he needs it. I guess what I mean here is that when the worker ends up doing something different from what you wanted, you've both goofed."

EXAMPLE: The Consequences of Misunderstanding

"Arinda, where are the pads I asked you to order?"
"I'll get them for you, Mr. Phillips. I picked them up at supply on my way into work this morning."
"How in the world could you carry three gross of pads?"
"Three *gross*? I thought you wanted me to get three pads!"

"Allen, do you have the Sabre proposal for me?"
"Yes, ma'am—right on schedule."
"What's this mess?"
"It's the proposal. Didn't you want to see it in draft?"
"Draft?! It's due in final form in Mr. Linkletter's office in half an hour."
"Gosh, Ms. Abrams. I'm really sorry, but I'm sure you told me you wanted to see a draft by this afternoon."

(**WHAT IF** you were Mr. Phillips or Ms. Abrams? What do you do now?)

"That sounds good, Amelia, but I'm not sure I see just how to do it."

Some Practical Tips

"Okay, let's practice it. I'm working for you, and you want me to do a price survey and buy a new copying machine for you. How would you do that as a complete delegation?"

"I think I understand. I'd say, 'Amelia, I want you to get us a new copying machine. Be sure you find the best price and try to get it here by about January 1.'"

"Good beginning, but you made two mistakes. First of all, you didn't tell me what kind of copier you want. If I'm a good worker—and I am, because you're making a complete delegation—I'll ask you for more details. But I really shouldn't have to do that. You should take the lead there.

"Second, you never delegate to someone to 'try' to do something, and there's no such date as 'about January 1.' If you mean 'I want you to purchase one and have it here by January 1,' say that. If you mean 'I'd like you to have it by January 1, and if you can't, tell me by December 15 when you can have it,' tell me that. Even if it's a complete delegation, don't leave the time target fuzzy. Does that make sense?"

"Yeah, Amelia, I see what you mean. Let me try another one."

"This time, let's say you want to accomplish the same thing, but you want to make the purchasing decision. How would you do that?"

"I'd say, 'Amelia, we need a new copier. I'd like to upgrade what we have, and I want to know what's available. Look over the market for a good buy and get back to me with your recommendation by December 15. On your way out, ask my secretary to put you on my calendar for then.'

"Now I know I would have given you a lot more details, and probably discussed any models that I had in mind with you. Can we just pretend I did that?"

"Okay—and this time you did well. I have a pretty clear idea of what you want me to do, and I know exactly when I need to have it done. The only thing I don't have is a good understanding of the range of alternatives you want to consider. You may want me to recommend one machine, or you may want to pick from three or four. It would be helpful for you to give me that information."

"I understand that—it makes sense."

"One more thing, Bill. Let's suppose that I walk in on the morning of December 15 and tell you I need another week. I've just had too many things piled on me. . . ."

"Whoa right there. That's when I'd put on my correcting hat and you and I would have a little heart-to-heart. I see what you mean about missing a time target. If I really needed that copier by January 1, I'd be in deep trouble."

"Exactly—and that's why you have to insist that people notify you in advance when they can't meet a time target. If you're expecting something to be done, and then you find out at the last moment it's going to be delayed, your planning is shot. You just don't let workers do that to you."

"Thanks, Amelia. I think I have the picture now."

Delegating Problem Solving

"You do, but I want to make one other point, and that's about problem solving. When they interviewed you for the management job, did they ask you how you were at problem solving?"

"They sure did. I don't think I'd have gotten the job if I hadn't convinced them I'm good at it."

"I expect you are good. And if you're not careful, it's going to foul you up."

"Huh? What do you mean?"

"Bill, what's your reaction if one of your workers brings you a problem?"

"Generally, I try to solve it for him on the spot. If I can't, I work on it for a day or two. If it can be solved, I can usually work it out by then."

"Okay—what does the worker learn from that?"

"He learns that I can be depended upon to solve problems."

"True. Doesn't the worker also learn that he can dump problems on you and not have to worry about them any more?"

"No, of course not . . . hmmm . . . I guess you're right. I do end up solving most problems for my people."

"They're really delegating upward, aren't they?"

"Wow! I never thought of it that way, Amelia. I guess so. Now that you put it in those terms, it doesn't sound like such a good thing for me to do."

"It isn't. Not only do you let them delegate work to you, but you keep them from learning how to solve problems themselves. If you have successful workers, you do something even worse: You keep the most interesting part of the work for yourself."

"You've made a believer of me—but how do I stop?"

"Basically, you delegate problem solving to your people. Your worker may be able to solve a given problem on the spot; often, when a worker turns to you for a solution he already has one and is hoping you'll ask for it. If he can't solve it, delegate the problem at a level you're comfortable with and treat it like any other delegation. You'll be helping to create a successful worker, *and* you'll keep some unnecessary work off your desk."[3]

EXAMPLE: Keeping Problems Where They Belong

"Mr. Anselm, I have a problem with the automatic feed on my machine. It keeps jamming."

"Have you tried to fix it?"

"Well, I checked for debris in the gears, but they're clean."

"What do you think is causing the jamming?"

"Well, Henry said that when he had this problem with a machine, it had something jammed back under the cam."

"Do you think you could check that?"

"Yeah, I think so. If that doesn't work, is it okay to take the cover off and check the shaft? . . ."

"Ms. Emory, we have a real problem. Supply will only send us two boxes of diskettes a week, and we're using almost three times that many. Can you talk to them?"

"Maybe. Have you tried borrowing disks from another section?"

"We've already borrowed everything we could find, and we've recycled all of our disks that don't have current data."

"Okay. I want you to draft a letter to Supply for me to sign. Give them the facts on what we're using and ask for whatever amount of diskettes you think we need. After I sign it, you can take it down there and work something out with them. . . ."

"Ms. Chastain, I have a problem. Tony Carlos keeps asking me to help him with his work, but he never wants to help me with mine."

"What would you like me to do, Elaine?"

"Tell Tony to help me."

"Do you think he would like that?"

---

[3] It's important to have your common sense up and running here. There are some problems you should solve. If a worker comes in and says "Charlie and Max are fighting in the break room," delegation probably isn't the appropriate response.

The touchstone you should use is whether the problem is directly part of your responsibility as a manager. If it isn't, delegate it. If it is, handle it—unless delegating all or part of it would help develop the worker.

"It doesn't matter whether he likes it or not. He ought to help me!"

"Tell you what I'll do, Elaine. I'll get together with you and Carlos right after lunch. You can tell him what you think, and we'll see what the two of you can work out. . . ."

(**WHAT IF** Ms. Chastain had agreed to talk to Carlos for Elaine? Who would have delegated to whom? Who would have gotten the blame if things didn't go the way Elaine wanted?)

"I'm really glad I ran into you, Amelia, but I don't want to forget anything. Do you mind if I try to summarize what you've said?"

"Not at all, as long as it's . . ."

A QUICK SUMMARY

1. There are three basic principles of successful delegating:

    a. Your primary goal is to delegate to your workers responsibility and authority for their work. Neither you nor your workers will be successful unless this point is clear to everyone.

    b. You should delegate only what people are ready to handle. This includes making delegations that stretch your people a little each time.

    c. You must keep track of your delegations and know their outcomes.

2. There are five basic rules for successful delegating:

    a. Be clear about what you're delegating. This is where the different levels of delegating come in. You can delegate completely, substantially, partially, minimally, or not at all.

        1. Complete delegation means telling the worker what to do and by what date to have it finished. He will only report to you that the work has been completed.

        2. Substantial delegation is like complete delegation, except that you want the worker to see you *before* he takes final action. That way, if he is not doing what you think should be done, the two of you can discuss the situation before a final decision is made.

3. Limited delegation means telling the worker what needs to be done and asking him to make recommendations to you. You make the final decision.

4. Minimal delegation means telling the worker how to do the job and when to do it. You shouldn't let anyone operate on this level for long.

5. No delegation means telling a worker that you'll decide whether you want something done and get back to him. Avoid this level whenever possible because, otherwise, *you* end up with all the work.

b. Be sure every delegation has a specific time target. This can be the date by which it's to be done, or the date by which you'll get a progress report or recommendation.

c. Make it clear that time targets *will* be met. If they can't, the worker must get back to you in plenty of time, not at the last minute.

d. It's never your responsibility to follow up and see how a worker is doing with his delegation.

e. You and the worker share the responsibility for understanding what's to be done. This doesn't mean that you get off the hook if you're not clear about what you want, but a good worker must make sure he knows what you want.

3. Let workers solve their own problems.

StretchMeter 7: DELEGATING

1. My goal is complete delegation to each of my workers.

NEVER   0   1   2   3   4   5   6   7   8   ALWAYS

2. My delegations are challenging to my workers in a helpful way.

NEVER   0   1   2   3   4   5   6   7   8   ALWAYS

3. I see that the delegations I make stay under control.

NEVER   0   1   2   3   4   5   6   7   8   ALWAYS

4. I use whatever level of delegation is appropriate.

NEVER   0   1   2   3   4   5   6   7   8   ALWAYS

5. I put specific time targets on all delegations.

NEVER   0   1   2   3   4   5   6   7   8   ALWAYS

6. I insist that time targets be met.

NEVER   0   1   2   3   4   5   6   7   8   ALWAYS

7. I set levels of delegation that don't require me to "pester."

NEVER   0   1   2   3   4   5   6   7   8   ALWAYS

8. My workers make sure that I'm clear when I delegate.

NEVER   0   1   2   3   4   5   6   7   8   ALWAYS

9. When workers bring me problems, I let the workers solve them.

NEVER   0   1   2   3   4   5   6   7   8   ALWAYS

10. My goal is complete delegation to each of my workers.

NEVER   0   1   2   3   4   5   6   7   8   ALWAYS

Delegating ASAP

1. If your goal as a manager isn't complete delegation to your workers, neither you nor they will be as successful as possible. Sit down with a notebook or several sheets of paper—one for each worker. Write down the highest level of delegation you're comfortable making to the first worker. Then list the obstacle(s) to delegating more completely to him. Now, put down at least one step you'll take immediately to start removing the obstacle(s). Continue for each worker.

2. You can fail to challenge your workers helpfully in either of two directions:

   You may be too conservative, and not delegate as much responsibility as they're ready to take. If this is what's happening, do the exercise in ASAP 1.

   You may be delegating more responsibility than your workers can handle right now. (You know this is happening when you have to keep interfering to see that they get things right.) Doing ASAP 3 will help with this. (And remember that the purpose of increased delegation is to challenge your workers—not intimidate them.)

3. Not making careful, controlled delegations is as harmful as not making delegations. Review the five levels of delegation. Then make a page for each worker (as in ASAPs 1 and 2). Determine the highest level of delegation you can give that worker and still be confident you have the delegation under control. Limit your delegations to him to that level—until you can develop that worker further (again, see ASAPs 1 and 2).

4. Review ASAPs 1, 2, and 3. One of them will help you select more appropriate levels of delegation.

5. When you don't put specific time targets on all delegations, you're setting the worker *and* yourself up for failure. Review the levels of delegation to see what time targets are appropriate at each level. Starting tomorrow, don't make a delegation below the complete level without setting a *specific* time at which the worker is to get back to you for the next step. Do it, without exception, until it becomes second nature.

6. Once time targets are set, they must be met. If you've been letting your workers fail to meet targets, call a meeting tomorrow. Tell your people that you're sorry you've been letting them down that way and explain that now you've seen the light. Let them know that, as of the end of the meeting, deadlines must be kept—period.

   Your group won't love you for this change, but you and they will function more effectively because of it.[4]

7. You don't have to "pester" when you make realistic delegations. Refer to ASAP 3.

8. It's your responsibility first to see that you're clear about what you want when you delegate, but it's in your workers' best interest to help you in this. The next few times you delegate to a worker, encourage him to ask you for all the details he needs. Stress that you want to be clear and you need his assistance. If you're honest about it, this technique will help.

9. When you solve problems for workers, you let them effectively delegate upward. Like Bill, you may need a Reaction Alert (see the ASAPs for Chapter 1). Put a ball right in the middle of your desk to remind you that when one of your people walks in with a problem the ball stays in his court. Either he solves it on the spot or he walks out with it as a delegation. You can help him with the problem—if that's appropriate—but see that you don't take over the problem.

10. See ASAP 1. The question is important enough to repeat.

---

[4]If you can't think of anything else, explain to them that the change will build character.

CHAPTER 10

Supporting

PHASE ONE MANAGEMENT	
Structuring	C O M M U N I C A T I N G
Selecting	
Guiding	
Correcting	
Motivating	
Delegating	
Supporting	

In this chapter, you'll find useful information on:

How important it is to support your workers.

How to convince your boss that your workers are successful and that *you're* successful.

How to protect your workers from harassment without "rescuing" them.

This chapter will help you develop successful workers by seeing that they have the tools and supplies *that they need. It will also explain how to support workers so they will consistently* take responsibility for their work *and* be motivated.

WHAT IS EFFECTIVE SUPPORTING?

Phillip McDonald (bangs on the vending machine until the bag of potato chips falls to the tray): You know, I'm getting burned out on Chris as a supervisor. He gives us all this jazz about doing a good job and then won't get us the stuff we need to do it.

Roger Dejarnier (gets a cup of coffee from another machine and heads for a table): That's a shame. Evelyn's just the reverse. She's a real change from our last boss, Kellar. I used to have to fight like crazy to convince him that we needed new versions of our drafting software. Now all I have to do is explain to Evelyn what a program will do, and she does her darnedest to get it for us. And you're right—that does make it easier to do a good job.

Phillip: I don't think the idea of helping us out ever crossed Chris's mind. We've been trying for months to persuade him to try to get us some better quality paper. It's useless—we're still using the standard junk that misfeeds more often than not.

Roger: Oh, I'm glad we don't have to put up with that. Evelyn gets us what we need and then stays out of our way. She comes by once in awhile and asks how I'm doing. If I don't have a problem, I say, "Fine." Then we talk for a little bit, and she goes on to someone else.

Phillip: It would be great if Chris were like that. He gives us something to do, and then he keeps looking over our shoulders while we do it.

Roger: It sure helps when someone believes you're smart enough to do a good job and doesn't hassle you. You know, I think the thing I like the most is the way Evelyn keeps the flack off us. Charlie Tuttle, from the design department came over here the other day and started telling me how to lay out my drawings. Before he got two sentences out, Evelyn came up—and the next thing I knew he was in her office. Later, she came back and asked me to make a couple of small changes. I was glad I didn't have to deal with Charlie and his temper.

Phillip: If anyone comes by our section yelling at us, Chris disappears. It's as bad here as it was down in the lab. Down there, half a dozen people were telling me how to run the tests. When I'd complain to Elsie, she'd just tell me to give people what they wanted. Some days I'd run the same test three different ways for three different people!

Roger: It helps when you get your orders from one person.

Phillip: I'd be grateful if Chris just stopped second-guessing us. About a year ago he had me negotiate a procedure change with R&D. I did it, but then Mr. Barker showed up over here with steam coming out of his ears—yelling about the new procedure we'd worked out. Chris flew out of his office and started yelling at me right along with him. Neither one of them paid any attention to what I had to say. Chris and Barker agreed on a different procedure right there—right there, without even asking me why I'd done it the way I had! Then Chris had the nerve to tell me to make the change and have it on his desk in an hour.

Roger: From what you say, I feel like giving Evelyn a medal. I remember shortly before she let Adrian go, when Adrian was making a lot of dumb mistakes. Evelyn tried and tried to get Adrian to change, but it was no use. Even then, Evelyn never let anyone from outside the section get after Adrian or tell her what to do.

Phillip: You're lucky to have a manager who does such a good job of supporting her people. Your only problem is, she's so good she's probably going to get promoted out of her job. Chris never will!

WHY IS EFFECTIVE SUPPORTING IMPORTANT?

Harold Ramsey learned quickly why it's important to support workers effectively. The first week on the job, he gave Ozzie McIntyre a special-purchase order and told him to expedite it. Ozzie did it, told Harold he had done it, and went about his business. Then Juanita Massey, who'd ordered the item, complained to Ozzie that the order wasn't what she'd wanted. Before Ozzie could answer, Harold walked up, apologized to Juanita for the fouled-up order and promised it wouldn't happen again. Then he took Ozzie into his office.

Ozzie, who was eligible for retirement, didn't feel he had to put up with anything from anybody. As soon as he was in Harold's office, Ozzie closed the door and turned on Harold in a rage.

"Don't you *ever* do anything like that again, or I'm out of here! I won't have you overruling me and embarrassing me in front of anybody—anybody!"

"Well, if you'd done it right," Harold replied angrily, "I wouldn't have had to do it! You know how important it is to keep our customers happy."

For the next five minutes, the two men had a shouting match. Things were going from bad to worse when Harold had the presence of mind to say, "Look, this is getting us nowhere. I'll shut up for a minute if you will, and then maybe we can talk about it." Ozzie glowered at him, but nodded. They sat down and looked at each other for a minute.

"Okay, Ozzie, I want to find out just what's eating you. If you'll stop yelling, I'll keep my mouth shut and listen."

Ozzie nodded, and told him: "Look, I know that wasn't just what Juanita wanted. But you told me to get the order expedited. It would have taken me four days longer to get her what she requested. So I did what you told me and bought the other."

Harold started to say something about pleasing customers again when he suddenly realized what Ozzie had just said. He grinned sheepishly, "I guess you did exactly what I asked you to do, didn't you?"

That got things back on an even keel, and Ozzie and Harold talked for quite a while. Then they got to the heart of the matter.

"Look," Ozzie said, "if you trust me enough to give me a job to do, then you ought to trust me enough to support what I do. At least you ought to listen to why I did something the way I did. You're the boss—I don't have any problem with that—and I like it when you let me use my own judgment. But I'm not going to do it if you're going to overrule me without listening to my reasons."

Harold did listen. When Ozzie left the office, both he and Harold felt good about their talk. As a matter of fact, Ozzie stayed on and worked for Harold for another five years before he retired. For his part, Harold learned some very important things:

1. The most important thing Harold learned was that if he expects employees to be successful, he has to give them the support they need. Without Harold's support, Harold's workers lose the motivation to be fully successful, and he loses credibility.

2. Harold learned that his workers were only behaving realistically. Without the right tools or supplies, without Harold's support, without protection from outside flack—his workers would waste tremendous amounts of time. It simply isn't worth it for them to take responsibility under those conditions.

3. And Harold learned that if he's going to manage the workgroup, he has to provide the support. It's important that the workers look to him and trust him to get them what they need and keep the flack off them. He has to make sure that other managers don't harass his people or give them work direction.

HOW DO I SUPPORT EFFECTIVELY?

Mary Ellen Zdenek: All right, you've read the chapter on supporting your workers, and we've spent the afternoon discussing how important it is. Now I want to know what you've gotten out of the book and the workshop that you're going to take back to the job.

Chris Turley: Frankly, I'm a little shaken up. I thought I was doing a decent job of supporting my people—but now I'm not so sure. The problem is I'm just not sure I can trust them. I can't support them unless I can count on them to do things right.

Evelyn Kee: It sounds to me like you need to go back and work on delegating effectively. I don't have any idea how good your workers are, but I know that if *you* don't think they're successful, you'll never support them properly. And you'll never know how good they are unless you delegate to them and see what happens.

Maria Vela: I'm going to work at delegating, too, but there's something else I'm going to do as well. I can see now that my workgroup needs to know what my philosophy is and how I want things done. There are lots of ways of doing things that are "right" in a vacuum, but they don't fit the way I want my people to do things. If I'm going to support them, I need to know in advance that what they do will be consistent with our overall approach as a team.

EXAMPLE: Communicating Your Philosophy

"Wynetta, let me say one thing right off: I'm very happy with the way you handled the joint report with Purchasing. I need to talk with you a little about it, but I want you to know that I'm not being at all critical."

"Mr. Ermina, that sounds like you're getting ready to zap me good."

"I'm sorry if it sounds that way because I'm not. In fact, what I want to do is to make up for a mistake on my own part. There's something about doing a joint report that I forgot to tell you."

"Okay. . . ."

"After you brought the report back to get it typed, you had a couple of good ideas that you had Ellen include in the final draft. The first time Purchasing saw those changes was when you took the final copy to them for signature."

"Yes, but they liked the changes."

"I know, but we can't count on that every time. One of the principles I always follow in a joint project is never to make a change unless both areas have agreed to it."

"I know that's good practice, but we were running late on the report, and I didn't want to hold it up."

"I understand your reasoning, but the principle is more important. We've spent a lot of time building up trust between us and the other sections. Part of that trust involves a promise that we won't even *appear* to do anything behind anyone's back."

"But I . . ."

"I know—you didn't intend to go behind Purchasing's back, and I don't think they took it that way. But you don't know how things were around here a couple of years ago when no one trusted anyone else. I don't want to do anything that might remind people of those days. And I know you don't want to, either."

"Oh, no—I really like the way we get along."

"We all do—so I want everyone in my section to be completely open in everything. Sure, it would have taken you a little longer to run those changes by Purchasing before you did the final copy. But it's important to take that time, and I want you to do it in the future."

"All right—I understand. The next time you give me a report to do, I'll make sure all changes get coordinated."

"Thank you. You're a good worker, Wynetta, and I really appreciate your flexibility. . . ."

(**WHAT IF** Mr. Ermina had just criticized Wynetta for not coordinating the changes? What do you think Wynetta's reaction would have been?)

Max Jaros: For me, I need to work on keeping out of my workers' way. They're good, and I've been interfering too much with them. I need to spend more time making sure that they get the supplies they need. We've had to go light on packing materials for the last two weeks, and several of my people have been complaining that they can't do a good job that way. I was out on the line, trying to help them—but I should have been finding out why there's a problem with the packing stuff, and fixing it.

Managing Your Boss

Evelyn: I think my biggest problem is my boss. He keeps wanting me to get involved in everything. If I tell him I've delegated some project and I know it'll be done right, he gets upset and insists that I get him a status report on it. Then when I ask the worker about the job's status, he gets upset because I don't trust him.

Maria: I used to have the same problem. Maybe your boss doesn't see you as a fully successful manager yet. If he'd read this book, he'd be working with you to make you successful. It doesn't sound like he is, so you've got to prove to him that you're successful. Tell me, do you make sure he knows it when one of your people does a particularly good job?

Evelyn: No, not really. I thought the idea was for him not to have to worry about my group.

Maria: You don't want him to worry about it, but I think you do want him to know how good it is. If you make it a point to keep him posted on your people's successes, he may start to realize how good they are. Then he won't have the same problem when you delegate fully to them.

Chris: Hey, that might work with formal recognition, too. I've never thought about it before, but when you give a worker an award for doing a good job, you're not just saying something to him. Other people—like your boss—see it, too. Of course, you can only pass out awards if your people earn them. . . .

EXAMPLE: Showing Off Good Workers

"Toni, it gives me great pleasure to recognize you as the Employee of the Month for our division. You're the third worker from your section to get the award in the last six months. I think that speaks well for you and your co-workers."

"Thank you, Ms. Feldman. It's a real pleasure to work in the division."

(A few minutes later.) "Well, Wilson, you did it again. Sometimes I think you have something on the judges."

"Not at all, Ms. Feldman. Frankly, it's all the result of that management course you sent me to about a year ago. What I learned there started me thinking about how capable my people really are. Each one of them who has won the award won it strictly on his own merit. I keep telling you how good they are; maybe now you'll start believing me."

"I must admit—you've become quite a salesman. But, I still find it hard to believe they're as good as you say they are."

"Let me tell you a secret. Do you remember how pleased you were with that design for the annual report? Well, Toni did that one."

"I expected you to do it yourself."

"I know. And if Toni hadn't done a good job, I would have—you don't ever need to worry about that. The point is that she did a super job. Neither you nor I needed to add a thing to it."

"Still, something that important . . ."

". . . Needs to be looked at carefully. I know that, and it was. It took me a while to realize it, but I have three or four people in my group who turn out first-rate work every time. Why should I waste my time looking over their shoulders or only give them the easy stuff to do while I take all the challenging material? Be honest, now—have you ever had such consistently good designs coming out of the shop before?"

"I hate to say it, but no. Your people *are* good. . . ."

(**WHAT IF** Wilson had never mentioned that Toni did the design for the annual report?)

Evelyn: It sounds funny, but if I understand all this correctly, one of my jobs is to convince my boss to make a complete delegation to me where my people are concerned. I've never thought of it that way.

Mary Ellen: That's a good insight. Remember, you're part of your boss's workgroup. Everything we've said about successful workers applies to you, too. You must show your boss that you know what to do and how to do it; you must have access to the proper tools with which to do it; and you must be certain that you and your boss agree on what constitutes doing your job well. Your boss needs to see that you're motivated and that you take responsibility for what your workgroup does.

Max: Yeah—this is all part of building up our credibility. Our bosses have to know that when we say we'll do something, we will—and that we'll do it well and on time. That's the only way we can keep them out of our hair.

Sarah Tillman: That's what I've been thinking about while I've been listening to all of you. My boss likes to get involved with my workgroup. She comes down to the section once or twice a day. If I'm there, we usually talk a little and she goes away happy. If I'm not, she'll find something about what my people are doing that she doesn't like and she'll tell them to change it. Then my workers get confused and don't know which way to do it.

Maria: I think we've all had that kind of boss, and it's a tough problem. If you tell your folks to ignore your boss, you'll really get into trouble. But if they listen to him you end up in just as much trouble. This is what I do: I tell my people to listen and make sure they understand whatever my boss is saying. Then, if they can, I ask them to hold off on *doing* anything differently until they check with me. That way, I get a chance to try to change my boss's mind if I don't like what he's done.

Max: That's a good idea. Tell me, Sarah, does your boss know how you feel about the way she goes around you to correct your people?

Sarah: To be honest with you, I've been afraid to bring it up. You've almost convinced me, though, that I need to talk to her and deal with this one head-on. My boss is pretty sharp; I think there's a good chance she'll listen.

EXAMPLE: Managing Your Boss

"Mrs. Cuellar, may I speak to you for a moment?"

"Certainly, Sarah—what's on your mind?"

"I don't know just how to put this. I hope what I have to say won't offend you."

"That bad, huh? Okay, let me have it."

"It's not *that* bad . . . it's just that . . . well . . . you keep telling my people what to do, and they're not sure which one of us to listen to."

"Sarah, I *am* their boss—and yours."

"I know you are, and so do they. Besides, it's not a question of disagreeing with what you say—we honestly want to do things the way you want them done. That's not really the problem, though. May I give you an example of what I mean?"

"Certainly."

"When you came by this morning, Gloria was classifying the warranty repairs. You stopped her and told her to change several of the classifications—remember?"

"Yes. The way she was doing it wouldn't have provided the kind of breakdown that the analysis group needs."

"I understand. Once Gloria told me what she was doing differently, I saw why you made the change. It does work better. The problem is that I'd told her to do it one way and then you came by and told her to do it differently. Gloria didn't know what to do; she was afraid she'd make one of us mad no matter what."

"That's unfortunate, but the repairs must be broken down the way I told her."

"Agreed. Remember, I'm not trying to argue with you about how to do the job. We *want* to do it your way. May I make a suggestion about how we could handle situations like this?"

"Go on."

"When you see a problem with the way someone in my workgroup is doing something and I'm not around, could you just ask the person to stop what he's doing and move on to something else until you have a chance to talk with me? Then you can tell me how you want it done, and I'll see that the worker makes the change. Then the worker won't have to worry about whom he takes instructions from or whom he might make mad."

"I'm willing to try it a time or two because I don't want to upset your people—but only if it doesn't hold things up."

"That's all I ask. I promise you—I'll make it work. . . ."

(**WHAT IF** Sarah hadn't said anything to her boss? Would it have affected Gloria's attitude toward Sarah as her boss?)

Protecting Workers

Furman Wright: It's not my boss that's my challenge in supporting my people—it's my customers. The organizational analysts all work for me, and they make a lot of decisions that aren't very popular. Not a week goes by that I don't walk into the office and find some other manager chewing on one of my people."

Sarah: I get some of that, too—probably we all do. How do you handle it?

Furman: Very carefully. On the one hand, I do delegate completely to most of my people. If they make a decision, I expect them to be able to defend it. I'm not about to rush in and try to rescue them; that's not good for anybody.

On the other hand, I absolutely will not tolerate someone abusing my people, particularly the newer ones. Just as soon as another manager begins to yell—and particularly if he starts getting personal—I take over. When my people become managers, they can put up with that; until then it's my job to protect them from that kind of abuse.

Maria: Good for you! I wish more managers felt that way. When you're a worker and somebody in management starts chewing on you, it's hard to know what to do. Because I've had some first-hand experience with that situation, I try my best to keep my people from ever getting caught in it. If I can't do that for them, none of the rest seems to matter much.

EXAMPLE: Preventing Abuse

"Dammit, Tim, you know I needed an answer today on that new function! I won't put up with this kind of garbage!"

"Mr. Wilson, I keep trying to tell you . . ."

"You keep trying to make excuses to me! I'm sick and tired of little wimps like you who think they can tell me what to do. Every one of you thinks they're better than the people who . . ."

"Sam, why don't you come into my office?"

"Dammit, Furman, keep out of this."

"No! I don't know what's going on here but it's completely inappropriate for you to talk to Tim that way. If you'll come with me, we can . . ."

"We can nothing—I've got some more things I want to say to your boy here."

"Well, you'll just have to go without saying them. Tim, why don't you take a break and step across the hall for a minute. Now, Sam, do you want to talk here or in my office or in my boss's office? . . . "

(**WHAT IF** Sam had wanted to go to Furman's boss's office? What approach should Furman take there?)

Mary Ellen: Very good—I can see that you all understand what you've read and that you've listened to each other. Let me see if I can capture the heart of it for us.

(She turned to a fresh sheet of paper on the easel and wrote . . .)

A QUICK SUMMARY

1. Important points in the chapter on supporting:
    a. If you expect your employees to be successful, you have to give them the support they need. Without that support, they lose motivation and you lose credibility.
    b. Employees are being realistic when they refuse to take responsibility without effective support.
    c. There's just as great a payoff for you. If you can't get your workers what they need, keep the flack away from them, and prevent other managers from giving them orders, you lose the ability to manage them.
2. Important points in the discussion:
    a. We must develop successful workers. We can't support them fully unless they're good.
    b. We must see that our workers know what our philosophy is and how we want things done.
    c. Once our people are successful, we need to stay out of their way. Our time should be spent supporting, not interfering.
    d. It's vital that workers have the right tools and supplies.
    e. We must convince our bosses that we're fully successful members of their workgroups. Until we do this, they'll continue to deny us the freedom we need to support our people effectively.
    f. We can improve our credibility by seeing that our bosses know when our workers do a good job. Recognizing workers formally also helps.
    g. We need to persuade our bosses not to give our people orders directly, but to go through us. If we don't, we put our workers in uncomfortable situations.
    h. It's our responsibility to protect our workers from abuse by others without trying to "rescue" them from supporting their own actions.

"May I try and summarize the whole thing in one sentence?" Maria asked.

"Certainly. Here's the marker."

Maria wrote:

In other words,

If you want your people to take responsibility for what they do, you've got to support them when they do it.

Everybody agreed.

StretchMeter 8: SUPPORTING

1. I support my workers even when things are tense.

NEVER   0   1   2   3   4   5   6   7   8   ALWAYS

2. My workers are so good that I can easily support them.

NEVER   0   1   2   3   4   5   6   7   8   ALWAYS

3. My workers know what my philosophy is.

NEVER   0   1   2   3   4   5   6   7   8   ALWAYS

4. My workers have the supplies they need to be successful.

NEVER   0   1   2   3   4   5   6   7   8   ALWAYS

5. My boss believes I'm a successful manager.

NEVER   0   1   2   3   4   5   6   7   8   ALWAYS

6. My boss gives orders to my workers through me.

NEVER   0   1   2   3   4   5   6   7   8   ALWAYS

7. I protect my workers from abuse.

NEVER   0   1   2   3   4   5   6   7   8   ALWAYS

8. I let my workers deal with honest criticism themselves.

NEVER   0   1   2   3   4   5   6   7   8   ALWAYS

Supporting ASAP

1. Workers take with a grain of salt what you say when things are going well. They believe what you say—and do—when the going gets tough. This one is a piece of cake: all it takes is intelligence and guts! Before you make any delegation, ask yourself, "Am I willing to support whatever this worker does?"[1] Make the fullest delegation you can and still answer "yes." That's intelligence. Then, delegate and support the result, no matter what. That's guts.[2]

2. The key to effective support is developing workers whose work makes supporting them easy. If you haven't done that yet, review the last six chapters and do the relevant ASAPs.

3. Passing on your philosophy to your workgroup is critical, but you don't have to call it a "philosophy." At the next six meetings you have with your full workgroup—no less often than once a month, surely— discuss some aspect of getting things done that's important to you. You might choose topics like "listening to customers" or "the impor- tance of careful proofreading" or "why the machinery needs to be spotless." The only requirement is that it must be something you genuinely care about and want your workers to practice.

4. No worker should have to do a job with inadequate tools, equip- ment, or supplies. If your people are hampered in this way, it's time to make a change. Compile a list of the four tools, pieces of equipment, or kinds of supplies that they need the most. Work on the first item on the list until you've arranged to get what your people

---

[1] Remember that "whatever this worker does" varies with the level of delegation. If its complete delegation, you've committed yourself to his decision—it's going to be your decision. With substantial delegation, you get a final shot at it before it goes out. If it's minimal delegation, you control both the decision and its implementation. Picking the appropriate level of delegation is the key.

[2] Remember, too, that supporting a worker doesn't mean that you uncritically accept what he does. If the end result isn't what you wanted, it's time to put on your correcting hat— but in private. Supporting the worker means that in public you fully support his action— and, if it has to be changed, you make it possible for *the worker* to change it.

need. Then do the second, then the third, then the fourth. After that, see what else remains. From then on, never let the list get longer than one item.

5. It's not impossible to be better than your boss thinks you are, but it is hard. For the next four weeks, point out at least one accomplishment of your workers to your boss each week. Two or three would be better. If you can't identify at least one accomplishment a week, go back to Chapter 8 and proceed from there.

6. It's challenging but necessary to find a way to keep your boss from giving orders to your workers directly. The example in this chapter is one approach; there are dozens of others. Choose one, and pursue it for the next few days or weeks. Make it clear to your boss that you want to cooperate fully—but that you also want to be the one who tells your workers what to do. While you're waiting for your boss to change, make sure that each worker knows to tell you as soon as he can whenever he gets instructions directly from your boss.

7. Your workers don't get paid to take abuse. You should believe that down to your toes and *practice* it. If you haven't been practicing it, right now is just barely soon enough to begin. Note that when Furman couldn't redirect Sam Wilson in the example in this chapter, he made it impossible for Wilson to continue being abusive by sending Tim away. Whatever the means, put yourself between your worker and the abuser and stay there. It's all part of having the guts mentioned in ASAP 1.

8. The other side of sheltering workers from abuse is letting them learn to deal with honest criticism. If you tend to jump in just because they're being criticized, stop. If it's a deeply ingrained habit, use a Reaction Alert (see the ASAPs for Chapter 1).[3]

---

[3]We're talking about trained workers here. Naturally, you don't make new, inexperienced workers defend themselves alone. The more you can let a worker carry the ball, though, the better. Then you can limit yourself to providing "moral support" and reinforcing his responses.

CHAPTER 11

Communicating, Part I

PHASE ONE MANAGEMENT	C O M M U N I C A T I N G
Structuring	
Selecting	
Guiding	
Correcting	
Motivating	
Delegating	
Supporting	

In this chapter, you'll find useful information on:

Being open and honest.

Being clear.

Listening.

Good communication skills are absolutely essential for developing successful workers. All managerial activities—structuring, selecting, guiding, correcting, motivating, delegating, and supporting—depend completely on effective communication for success.

WHAT IS EFFECTIVE COMMUNICATING?

"**W**ell," said Helen Washington, "here we are."

"Yes, and we'd better get down to business," Clarice Kersey responded. "Imagine, giving us two hours to write an entire chapter."

Larry Malone grinned. "What's new? We never get enough time to do anything else. Why should this be different?"

"Then let's stop talking about it and *do* something," Fred Bernstein said. "I think communicating is the most important skill for a manager to have, and I think we ought to start there."

"You won't get any argument from me." The last speaker was Paula Macias, who had driven in from the suburban office. "Structuring, selecting, guiding, correcting, motivating, delegating, and supporting are all important—but if you can't communicate well, you can't do any of them effectively. Does everybody agree with that?"

They all nodded.

"I agree," Helen said. "Frankly, I didn't want to come to this meeting. But now that I'm here, I think that first of all an effective communicator is open and honest. It wastes too much time when people have to guess at what you're really after."

"But don't overlook clarity," Clarice added. "Everything needs to be put clearly and simply, whether you're speaking or writing."

"I heard what you said," Larry joined in, "and I think you both made important points. I'd like to add listening responsively to openness and clarity. If we're really going to communicate, I need to hear what you're saying—and I need to *show* you that I'm hearing it.

Fred nodded. "I'm hearing some very constructive ideas from the group. I'd like you to consider a fourth one: using feedback. It's hard to manage well if you can't give people an objective evaluation of what they do or say."

Paula leaned forward in her chair: "That's all well and good, but you're still missing something important. You've got to get in there and just persuade people sometimes. I believe in the value of being persuasive, and I'm sure each one of us sees its benefits."

WHY IS EFFECTIVE COMMUNICATING CRITICAL?

"Have you ever stopped to think," Charlie asked, "just how critical communicating is? There's not a single management activity that is effective unless the manager communicates effectively. Can you imagine trying to guide or delegate if you're not being clear, or correcting someone if you can't give objective feedback?"

"That's very true," Helen commented, "and it's true at every step. If a manager isn't open and honest, for instance, workers spend a tremendous amount of time trying to figure out what's really going on. Several years ago when I worked in a district office of another company, there was a lot of talk about a reorganization. Our manager wouldn't tell us anything, so we assumed that we were about to lose our jobs. Each one of us started looking for another position, and a couple of people actually left. Then we found out that the reorganization wasn't going to touch the district offices. It was never the same there again, though, and I left a couple of months later.

"I'd like to make a speech about how important being clear is, but I don't think I have to," Clarice said with a smile. "Let me try something else. Raise your hand if you *haven't* had a worker do something wrong in the last two months because you weren't clear about an assignment."

No hands went up. "Case closed."

"We've been talking about the output side of communicating," Larry added, "but don't forget the listening side. One frequent complaint I've heard from workers over the years is 'My boss won't listen to me.' That really bothers people. I'll bet each of us has had the same problem with our own bosses." Almost everyone nodded. "I thought so. What do you do when your boss won't listen?"

"I'll tell you what you do," said Paula. "You stop talking. What good does it do you to tell someone something you think is important if he won't listen to you?"

"Exactly. Nothing else works if the person isn't listening."

Fred leaned forward: "I find this very useful, and I'd like to add something to it. Effective communicating requires listening, all right, but that's not enough. You also need to feed what you hear back to the person speaking. That way, you can check to make sure that what you heard is what the other person said. If the two of you don't use feedback, you may have completely different ideas—yet think you're agreeing."

"Like that old Abbot and Costello routine, 'Who's on First?' At the end they agree, but each of them is saying something completely different." Helen grinned as she mentioned it.

"Yeah, I remember that. But there's more. If you don't give feedback to workers on what they're saying and doing, they never know when they make mistakes," Helen said emphatically. "When I took over my section two years ago, there was a guy in it who I was told was incompetent. I did have to spend some time working with him, but in a matter of weeks he improved to a fully satisfactory rating. Do you know what the real problem was? Nobody had ever told him that what he was doing wasn't okay. And I've seen the same thing time and time again—all from lack of feedback."

"I don't want to argue with any of you," Paula said as she gestured vigorously, "but you're still leaving out something critical. Where would any of us be if we weren't persuasive? What do you do when being open and clear fails—fire the poor worker? Not me, anyway. I'd certainly rather try to persuade him to do things my way. Wouldn't you each agree that persuasion is a critical part of communicating?"

Everyone nodded, and then Helen added, "Paula, I know how important you think persuasion is—and I think it's important, too. But we have to be careful not to rely on it in isolation. Combined with openness, responsive listening, and feedback, it's very useful. But if you try it without the others, you can get yourself into a situation where you don't know what's going on in your own workgroup."

Paula began, "Now wait a minute. . . ."

"It's okay, Paula," Fred interrupted. "Helen thinks persuasion is important, just like the rest of us. It's just that by itself, persuasion is all one way. A manager who's always pushing his own ideas doesn't hear what workers are trying to say. Problems that might otherwise surface stay hidden because people believe the manager isn't interested. It's not that persuasion doesn't matter—it's just that it needs to be part of an overall balance. Right?" He looked at the others. They nodded emphatically, and even Paula agreed.

HOW DO I COMMUNICATE EFFECTIVELY?

"You're right," Paula said. "I know how important these other qualities are. It's just that I had it drilled into me that I had to be a good salesperson in order to be a successful manager. Now I know that's not enough, but it made such an impression on me that it's still the first thing that comes to mind.

Being Open

"Yes, I remember that seminar," Helen said with a wry smile. "They should have put us through it *after* they told us about everything else. If there's one thing I think I've learned, it's that you can't be an effective manager if your people don't trust you. And they're not going to trust you if you're not open and honest with them."

Larry joined in, "You bet! I wrestled with this a long time myself. I had the idea that because *I* was the manager *I* was the one who had to have all the answers. I never let my workers know if I was having problems, and I never admitted it to them if I was wrong and they were right. When I finally gave in to the obvious and just started being myself, it made all the difference in the world."

"Yes, being open to what others have to say is very important," Helen said. "It's a part of the listening that Larry was talking about, but it's a part of openness, too. It means you have a real give-and-take with your workgroup and let yourself change. Do you know the remarkable thing about all this? If your workers realize you're willing to change, they become a lot more willing to change themselves."

Fred nodded: "That's good. I think I heard you say that openness means:

1. Being yourself and not playing some kind of role. You let your workers in on what's happening inside your head. If they ask questions, you give them the most honest answers you can. That way, they can trust what you say and don't have to second-guess you.

2. Being receptive to what your workers have to say and willing to take them seriously. If you have to change some of your ideas, that's okay.

Your goal is what's best, not what's 'yours.' When your people see that you're open to them, they can be open with you—which makes it easier for them to change if that's necessary.

"Did I get it right?"

"You certainly did," Clarice said enthusiastically, "but if this is going to be part of a book for managers, I think we need to add something here. If you inherit a workgroup that's not accustomed to honesty and openness, don't expect them to change overnight. Be as honest and open as you can and give them the chance to be the same. But give them some time to see that they can really trust you. Be patient and consistent, and they'll come around."

"I agree. It took a very long time for my group to communicate openly," Helen said, "but it was certainly worth it."

EXAMPLE: Being Open

"I'm sure that our managers will do what's best for us. Now let's just forget our questions and put in a good day's work."

or

"I don't know whether we'll be affected by the district office consolidations. Frankly, I'm as concerned as you are. I promise you, I'll let you know if I find out anything."

"It's not up to you to question my decisions. If you get to be a manager someday, you can make the decisions. Until then, just do it my way."

or

"I realize that my approach on this may not be the best. But right now, it's the best way I know to get it done. If someone has another idea that we could implement quickly, I'm willing to listen. If not, I expect you to do it this way."

"Okay, here are the objectives and the milestones for the Mendoza project. I expect everyone to get his part of the job done on time. Now let's get to work."

or

"Here's a draft of the plan for the Mendoza project. I want each of you to look at the part that you'll be working on and let me know by this afternoon whether or not you think the milestones are realistic. We'll get back together as a group tomorrow morning to iron out the details."

(**WHAT IF** you took the first option of each pair of examples? What would the workers' reactions be? How would they be different if you chose the second options?)

Being Clear

"Yes—there's no substitute for openness. In a different way, being clear is just as important. When I first came to work here, I thought I would never understand all of the technical terms and abbreviations we use. Then one day soon after I became a manager, I was explaining what we do to my first new hire. My initial reaction to the blank look on her face was that she wasn't as smart as I'd thought. Then I realized I was using all the jargon that had given me so much trouble in the beginning, and that's when I became a convert to clear, simple English."

Paula nodded emphatically. "Amen! Nobody ever confused anyone by speaking and writing plain English. I get so fed up with the bureaucratese we write around this place. Just once I wish someone would say 'used' instead of 'utilized' or would just come out and recommend something, rather than 'it is recommended that. . . .'"

"Amen to your amen. I think being clear and simple is so much a part of being open and honest. How in the world can someone trust you when you sound like an operations manual?" Helen grimaced as she said these last two words.

"Do any of you ever compose your letters out loud before you write them?" Larry asked. Several of the others nodded. "I'm glad I'm not alone. It really helps me put my ideas into simple English, but I thought maybe I was being weird."

"Not at all," Fred said intensely. "Getting rid of jargon, speaking simple English, saying your sentences out loud before you write them—anything that will help you be clear is good. Do you know what I discovered the other day? When Ms. Jenks, the division chief, has a letter she's sending to all the employees, she gives it to the person who delivers the in-house mail and asks him to tell her what it says. If he can't understand it, she rewrites it. That's what she thinks of clarity and simplicity!"

EXAMPLE: Being Clear

"We have received your letter, subject as above, and considered the suggestions therein carefully. Our analysis reveals that the proposal which you bring forward, while not without considerable merit, does not integrate well with our current strategy."

or

"Thank you for your letter suggesting that we use videodiscs to advertise our products. It's a good idea, but we just can't use it right now."

"Charlie, you know that we think very highly of you around here and appreciate the numerous contributions you've made to the organization. However, I've been evaluating your production for the past few months, and while there are many, many instances of satisfactory production—indeed, some even better than satisfactory—there are also some instances, some few instances, of, shall we say, somewhat-less-than-satisfactory performance. While I don't want to exaggerate the importance of these, it does appear that . . ."

or

"Charlie, you don't usually make mistakes, but you've been making a lot of them lately. Why?"

"Our next award goes to a lady who embodies in herself the fine traditions that we have always tried to uphold here in the division—initiative, perseverance, innovation, and a full commitment to her job. It's difficult to find the words to express my admiration for her accomplishments and the high regard in which I hold her contribution to our organization. It is an honor, though, to be able to stand here today and recognize her sterling contribution to the success we've enjoyed over the past few months. I'm referring, of course, to . . ."

or

"Our next award goes to Nancy Weedam, who spearheaded the 30 percent productivity increase we've had in the last six months. I want her to come up here and tell us how she did it. . . ."

(**WHAT IF** you had just landed here from an alien planet? Would your intergalactic translator be able to unravel the meaning of the first statement of each pair in this Example?)

Listening

"Well, we certainly agree on the importance of clarity. Now if only the person who puts what we say into the book can make it clear to the readers. . . ."

"Yes," Larry commented. He paused a moment, then continued, "You know, though, whoever does that is at a real disadvantage because he can't hear what we're saying. Once we write down the words, all the nuances fall out. It's to our advantage that we work so closely with our workgroups. We can actually *listen* to them instead of having to read about what they think and feel, which sure makes a difference."

"Yes," Paula agreed, "but only if you let the person *know* you're listening. A worker can't see inside your mind, so you have to show your interest. If you lean back in your chair, fold your arms, and just say 'Hmmm' every so often, he'll never believe you're paying attention—no matter how carefully you're listening. You've got to lean forward, make eye contact, and respond to what the worker is saying if you want to show you're really listening."

"That's valid," Helen said, "as long as no one gets the idea that you have to do those particular things." Paula started to interrupt, but Helen continued, "No, no—I know you didn't mean that. We just need to make sure that whoever reads this knows that there are any number of ways for a manager to communicate that he's really listening. You know, something so simple as a raised eyebrow or a small gesture can show someone you're with him."

Larry looked at her and nodded. "Exactly—anything that shows you're really listening is okay. And don't forget to ask questions. You learn a lot more that way, and you communicate that you're interested in what the worker is saying. Besides,"—a sly grin crept over his face—"there's no better way to keep somebody from feeding you a line than to keep listening and keep asking questions."

"I had a beautiful example of that just yesterday," Fred said, grinning back at Larry. "Some of you know Frenchy Modisette over in Section A. Well, he came over here raising Cain about a report we'd done on a joint project. I didn't think he had anything to complain about, and I darned near told him so. But I kept listening—and asking questions—and finally the real problem came out. He thought we hadn't given him enough credit for some of the research he did. That was easy enough to change, but if I hadn't held on and listened, I'd never have found out what was wrong.

EXAMPLE: Listening

"I'm through, Andy—done, finished! I've had it with this place! I quit!"

"Wow. What happened, Graham?"

"I don't even want to talk about it. I just want out!"

"It must have been pretty bad."

"It was. No matter how hard you work around here, they never show you any respect. Never!"

"Did something go wrong with the new automated cataloging system you've been developing?"

"Not something—someone. Actually, several someones. You'd think I'd never installed a system in my life, from the way they talked to me."

"Mrs. Shields didn't like the modification?"

"She never saw it. I was trying to bring it up when the terminal died on me, and I couldn't bring it back. They started making comments, as if it were my fault and I didn't know what I was doing."

"It sounds like they were pretty rough on you."

"That's putting it mildly."

"It also sounds to me like you got pretty frustrated with the system yourself."

"I did. I'm so tired of these ancient terminals. They should have been turned in two years ago. Instead . . ."

(**WHAT IF** Andy had just taken Graham at his word when he said he didn't want to talk? What would have happened? How would Graham have felt an hour later?)

"Listening is very important," Fred continued, "and there's something else useful you can . . ."

There was a loud knock and the door opened. Reggie Rosenfeld stuck his head in and said, "You'll have to leave. We have the room reserved for the rest of the day."

"That's a fine kettle of fish," Paula responded. "Just where do you think we can go?"

"Well, the easiest thing would be just to move to the next chapter. It's empty."

"I guess we could—but what about all the stuff we've written on the blackboard? Do we have to copy it and write it up again?"

"No," Fred said emphatically. "This is a book and we can do anything we want. Let's just take the blackboard with us. . . ."

CHAPTER 12

Communicating, Part II

PHASE ONE MANAGEMENT	C
Structuring	O
Selecting	M
Guiding	M
Correcting	U
Motivating	N
Delegating	I
Supporting	C
	A
	T
	I
	N
	G

This chapter contains the rest of the information about the importance of communication:

Giving and receiving feedback.

Being persuasive.

Nothing has changed much since the last chapter. Good communication skills are absolutely essential for developing successful workers.

THE DISCUSSION RESUMES

Giving Feedback

F red hung the blackboard on the wall and closed the door behind the others. "As I was saying, there's something else useful you can do when you're listening, and it's one of my main concerns: feedback. If you reflect back to the speaker what you heard, you show that you're listening *and* you give him a chance to correct you if you misunderstood. I don't think it's possible to be clear or to listen effectively without feedback."

"Will it surprise you if I agree with you completely?" Paula asked. "One of the big mistakes people make when they're trying to persuade others, is talking most of the time. Nothing turns people off quicker than that. The worse thing is, you never know it . . . Well, actually you do know it—but not until later when you find out you screwed up."

Fred tapped Paula on the shoulder. "Right! The first time I heard about feedback, I realized I rarely used it. So, I set myself goals for more than a month to make sure I gave people feedback. I actually kept a record. For the first week, I did it at least five times a day. By the end of the month, I was up to 10 to 20 times a day. Boy, did that ever help! Now, it's the most natural thing in the world for me to do."

"I won't say 'Amen,'" Clarice told him, grinning, "because I don't want this to sound like a prayer meeting. But it's true. You know, an important part of giving feedback is remaining objective and not getting involved and judgmental. If you sound like you're accusing the other person of something when you give feedback, he'll have the opposite reaction from what you want."

"Yes," Helen agreed. "When you can give feedback objectively, you can give the people you work with useful responses. This is especially important when you have to provide correction to workers on their performance or conduct.

"Some of my workers have told me that I used to sound very judgmental when I talked with them about improving their performance. It's no wonder I didn't get anywhere! Now, I sit down and try to discuss their work with them objectively, as if we were talking about how to hang a picture or prune a tree. It works, too."

"Do you know why?" Paula jumped in. "When you use a judgmental approach, you sound as though you're attacking the *person*. When you remain objective, you can talk about what the individual *did*, not what he is. I think that's so important because feedback isn't judging or evaluating someone else. It's giving him useful information about how you see his ideas or his work or his behavior. You can be completely objective and still do it effectively."

EXAMPLE: Giving Feedback

"Bertha, you're just not applying yourself. I don't know what's the matter with you. Your work used to be so good, but now it's barely satisfactory. I don't think you care about things any more."

or

"Bertha, the quality of your work seems to be falling off. What's wrong?"

"Ms. Kersey, you're not being fair to me in the way you're assigning work."

"And I don't think you're being very fair to walk in here and accuse me of that. Is that how a good employee should behave?"

"Well, I hate to complain, but it's been bothering me. I really don't feel . . ."

"I'm sorry if you're bothered, but you'll just have to accept the fact that we're all very busy right now."

"But . . ."

or

"Ms. Kersey, you're not being fair to me in the way you're assigning work."

"I'm sorry you feel that way. How am I being unfair?"

"I always get the jobs that require the most calculations. The others don't have to calculate nearly as much as I do."

"So you think that I'm assigning you the jobs with the most calculations because I'm unfair?"

"Yes—I don't know why else you'd do it. I hate to . . ."

(**WHAT IF** you used the second response to each pair of examples instead of the first? How do you think the worker would react? How would his reaction differ if you used the first?)

Dealing with Defensiveness

"You know, Paula, I'm getting a completely different picture of you from the one I had. You're not the glib salesman I thought you were. Actually, I guess you're not a sales*man* at all." Everyone laughed with Helen at the way she accented the statement. "But I want to ask the group something: What do you do with someone who gets defensive when you give him feedback, and he reacts as though you're criticizing him?"

"That's a good question," Fred responded, "and I don't have a pat answer. But I can tell you some of the things I do:

> First of all, it doesn't do you any good to attack the person. When someone gets defensive, it's very easy to start verbally beating him over the head. All that does, though, is make him even more defensive.
>
> Second, if you can, ask the person to explain what he's reacting to. When someone is defensive, it's because he thinks you're attacking him in some way. If you can get the person to tell you why he feels like he's being attacked, you have a chance to reassure him, and to communicate what you're trying to get across.
>
> Third, if it's your boss or another manager who's getting defensive, you may have to back off and try again some other time. But keep doing the other things we've been talking about: Be open, honest, and clear; and listen responsively. When you act this way, most people will start to trust you. Then they'll be more open to what you have to say.
>
> If it's a worker, you may want to back off for awhile, too. But there's one more thing involved in this case. A worker should understand that giving performance feedback is part of your job, and listening to it and using it is part of *his* job. It's part of being a successful worker— and it's almost impossible to be successful without it.
>
> And that brings me to the last point. If you want people to accept feedback from you, you should ask them to give feedback to you— and ask them sincerely. Nothing's a one-way street. One of the luckiest things that can happen to you is to find someone who will tell you honestly how he thinks you're doing.

If you do find someone who'll give you objective feedback, great—but don't count on it. If the only way you can get feedback is by letting someone yell at you, then do it that way. The important thing is to look for the feedback, make it clear that you want it, and accept it.

"There, that's what I know about handling people who get defensive when they're given feedback."

"Would you agree with something?" Larry asked. "A person can accept feedback and use it without having to agree with it, can't he?"

"Certainly—and I'm glad you added that. Neither you nor a worker has to accept another's feedback uncritically, but you should listen to it. If you don't understand it, or it doesn't sound right, ask questions. Think about it. Accept it as useful information, then decide what use to make of it."

"May I give you an example?" Clarice asked. "Just yesterday, one of my people told me I wasn't being fair with her in the way I assigned work. I was really tempted to jump on her because she's not one of my best workers—but I didn't. It turned out that she was uncomfortable doing calculations. I took care of that, but I used her feedback in another way, too. What she said helped me realize that I haven't been paying enough attention to my group's training needs lately."

"That's a good example—thanks," Helen said. "Let me try to tie defensiveness to something we were talking about a bit earlier. Defensiveness is caused by fear. People get defensive when they think someone is attacking them or trying to take something away from them. As a manager, the more open you are, the easier you are to trust. I don't disagree with anything anyone has said, but in the long run the best way to deal with defensiveness is to be open and trustworthy."

EXAMPLE: Dealing with Defensiveness

"Dorothy, we need to talk about your production."

"Oh, has somebody been complaining to you that I'm not carrying my share of the load, Mrs. Washington?"

"Actually, no one needed to. I can tell from the production figures, which I'll be glad to show you if . . ."

"Don't bother. I *knew* you were going to hassle me."

"No, I don't want to hassle you at all—but we do need to talk about your output."

"Sure, and how many others have you talked to about their 'output'? I'll bet you haven't talked to anyone else!"

"It doesn't really matter, does it? What's important to us is *your* production."

"Okay, here it comes. Preach me the sermon."

"I don't have to . . . Wait a minute, Dorothy. What's really bothering you about all this?"

"*You're* bothering me, picking on me like this. You're just like the others. I can't do anything right!"

"I'm sorry to hear that. I think you can be a good worker. Does it seem to you that I don't?"

"You've been so hard on me lately. I think you believe I'm no good at all."

"I know it's painful to feel that way. Is that why you don't want to talk about your performance?"

"I . . . I'm afraid you're going to tell me you're going to fire me. . . ."*

(**WHAT IF** Helen had gotten angry when Dorothy got defensive? What would have happened to the discussion?)

---

*Many of the examples in this book are compressed in time. Most incidents in real life take longer to develop. That's particularly true of this one. Defensiveness is often a deep-seated personal characteristic that doesn't change in a few words or sentences. A manager would be very lucky to get an employee to talk about his real fears as quickly as the one in this example did.

That doesn't mean the example is useless. If you deal with others with honesty and concern, it can—and usually will—help them be less defensive. Just expect it to take longer than it did in this example.

Persuading

There was a pause. Paula broke it with, "Okay, we've covered the other communication skills. Is it all right if I talk about persuasion now?"

She looked around. Most of the others grinned at her, and they all nodded. "Good! I don't want to downplay anything anyone has said. I hope I've convinced you that I believe those skills are important, too. But now that I've said that, let me also say that no manager's communication skills are complete until he's a good persuader."

"Look how often you have to use persuasion: getting your people to put in overtime when they don't want to; convincing them to try a new method; persuading your boss to let you run things your way; trying to influence another manager to put your group at the top of his priority list for supplies or work. The list goes on and on—don't you agree?"

"Yes," Helen responded, "we really do have to be persuasive. Keep in mind, though, that if we have an effective, open relationship with our workgroups, we'll spend more time trying to solve problems with our workers and less time trying to persuade them to do what we want. The same thing applies when we have good relationships with other managers and our bosses. Most of the times we need to use persuasion are those when we don't have a good relationship."

"Hmmm . . . Okay, I'll buy that," Paula said. "If I stop and think about it, that's one time when I have to use persuasion myself. There's another instance, too: when you want to make a quick decision and there's no time to work the situation through with everyone and develop a consensus. This is particularly true if the decision involves a significant change. To get the support you need in that kind of situation, you'd better be quite persuasive.

"I really do know that being open, communicating clearly, listening responsively, and using feedback are all part of being persuasive. But persuasion involves even more—can you agree with me on that?"

There was a pause, and then most of the group nodded. "Maybe we haven't paid enough attention to persuasion," Larry said. "What do you have to do to be persuasive?"

Paula smiled. "The very first thing is the one most people overlook: You have to *know who your audience is and what's important to them.* That applies whether you're working with an individual worker or dealing with a room full of executives. The more you know about your audience, how they think, how they feel, what they want—the more persuasive you can be. And, Larry, although you don't just do this by listening, listening responsively can be an important part of it."

Larry nodded.

Paula continued, "Knowing your audience isn't something you only do *before* you try to persuade them. You keep trying to understand them better by getting their reactions as you go along. You ask for feedback, you watch their body language—whatever clues you can get. If you don't, you have no idea how they're reacting; you can lose them completely and not realize it."

"You know I'm going to agree with you there," Fred said.

"I suspected it. Now, though, let's go to the second requirement: You've got to be able to *show your audience how what you want them to do will help them meet their important goals.* You want them to see that . . ."

Helen interrupted. "Paula, that sounds terribly manipulative to me. I'm not sure I could do it."

"I think you may be misunderstanding Paula here," Fred said to Helen. "When I was shopping for a television set a few weeks ago, I went to half a dozen places. The first five were all alike; the salespeople asked me what kind of set I wanted and how much I wanted to pay. Then they showed me everything they had anywhere close to that price range.

"The man at the last place I went to was different. He spent two or three minutes asking me just how I was going to use the set. Then he showed me three models. He explained the differences among them, told me how much each of them cost, and asked me what else he could tell me about them. You've probably guessed that that's where I bought my set. And I think that's the kind of persuading Paula is talking about—at least I hope so."

"It is, and thank you. What you've said ties right into the third thing you need to keep in mind: *the best persuasion is the selling that the other person does inside himself.* You give your audience all they need to know—and, let's be honest, you put the best face on it you can—then you let them take over. Pushing too hard is the worst thing you can do. As much as I believe in persuasion, I think high-pressure selling is the pits. I get my satisfaction from believing that I've done someone a service. By the way, that's exactly how I look at it when it's my own workgroup or another manager that I'm trying to influence."

"That sounds like 'persuading with integrity,'" Helen said. "I think I can agree with that."

"Me, too," Clarice added, "but let me add one other idea. I remember reading a long time ago that one of the best recruiting devices was a good reputation—and I think that's true of persuasion, too. *You influence people a lot more by what you are than what you say.* If they think you're a solid, trustworthy person whom they can depend on, they'll be a lot easier to persuade. If they think you're trying to put one over on them, you're doomed."

"Thank you," Paula said, "I really appreciate your adding that. In the long run, it's what we are that persuades people—or doesn't persuade them. That's what ties persuasion in with the other characteristics. Even in the most superficial relationships, where you have to depend on persuasiveness most heavily, the kind of person you are starts to show through. As the old saw puts it: 'What you are speaks so loudly that they can't hear what you say.'"

EXAMPLE: Persuading

"I stopped work early today and called you together for a specific reason. Some of you are really against the idea of doing a just-in-time inventory system for the branch. I understand why you're concerned. I know you're all thinking about what happened in Building 3. I admit that was a mess but I've looked into it, and I don't think we have anything to worry about. They weren't ready to do the system, and we are.

"In fact, this could be a real opportunity for us. We've worked hard for the last year to get Division to recognize the good job we do. If we put in a just-in-time system and it works—and it will work, believe me—we'll show everybody just how good we are.

"I want you each to think about that. We'd be the first unit in the Division to implement just-in-time successfully. Ask yourself how it would feel to have people saying that about you.

"For some of you, it may boil down to this—I'm asking you to trust me. I've looked the proposal over carefully, and I'm convinced we can make it work. I don't think I've ever let you down before, and I promise you I won't this time. . . ."

(**WHAT IF** the manager had more time available to deal with the idea of a just-in-time inventory system? What else might he have done to "sell" the idea?)

Some Tips

There was a long pause while everyone digested the discussion. Then Larry spoke, "Can I add one more thing? How you communicate makes a tremendous difference. When I think about all we've said, it really seems to me that the more informal the communication, the better. I know I prefer face-to-face discussions, like this one. Putting something in writing really inhibits me."

"I agree," Helen commented, "and there's one situation where I think this is especially true. All of us have to deal with the unpleasant aspects of our jobs—you know, giving performance appraisals to poor workers, correcting workers who don't want to be corrected, dealing with angry managers or customers. It's a tremendous temptation to duck the unpleasantness of a one-on-one and communicate in writing. I can tell you from hard experience, though, that's a poor way to operate."

"Yes it is," Clarice replied, "and it's particularly a poor way to operate when you're dealing with a union. Just as there are all kinds of unions, there are all kinds of relationships between unions and management, and even the best of them can get tense. It's oh so easy to put everything in writing and 'let 'em do what they want with it'—but it doesn't work. It's amazing how much you can accomplish, even if the overall relationship is bad, if you're willing to deal honestly with the steward face-to-face."

"It is," Fred said, "but it takes time. If you think you have to be patient when you're getting workers to trust you, just try it with a suspicious union steward. I've been in my job over a year, and the steward is just now reaching the point where she'll come and talk to me instead of firing off a grievance. She wouldn't admit it, but it's already made life easier for both of us."

"Well, folks, it's been charming—but it's also been long. I need to get back to my office and take care of some things, and I expect you do, too." Paula looked around questioningly, and several of the others nodded.

"Can I suggest that we each write down the points that were most important to us. Then we can read them to each other and make any additions. When we're finished, we'll pass them along to whomever called this meeting in the first place."

"Good idea, Paula." Clarice got the pads and pencils from the center of the table, passed them around, and they all began writing.

When it looked like everyone was done, Paula spoke up again. "Let's go around the table, and each person will give . . ."

A QUICK SUMMARY

They did, and this is what they worked out:

1. *Being open and honest* is the first characteristic of an effective communicator.
   a. If a manager isn't open and honest, people waste time and energy trying to guess what's really happening.
   b. Effective management requires trust. People will trust those who are open and honest with them.
   c. Openness means two different things:
      1. The manager acts genuinely and doesn't play some kind of role.
      2. The manager is open to input from others. The goal is what's best, not what's "yours" or "mine."
   d. When there is a real give-and-take in the workgroup, people become more willing to change.

2. *Communicating clearly* is the next characteristic.
   a. When a worker doesn't do what was asked, it's probably because the manager wasn't clear.
   b. Nothing communicates better than clear, simple English. Jargon and "bureaucratese" are confusing to people who don't use them all the time.
   c. A manager should take steps to see that what he writes is clear.
      1. Compose out loud to see how things sound before writing them down.
      2. Test what's been written by showing it to an "average" reader and clarify anything that's misunderstood.
   d. Being clear and simple is a necessary part of being open and honest.

3. *Listening responsively* means a manager doesn't just listen but *shows* the other person that he's paying attention.
   a. A good listener is a *responsive* listener, not a passive one.

    b. A good listener leans forward, makes eye contact, gestures—whatever is needed to show that he is hearing the other person.

    c. A good listener asks questions, which helps him learn, and shows interest in the subject.

4. *Using feedback* is essential for successful communication.

    a. Without feedback, a manager never knows whether he is being heard accurately. Two people who think they're agreeing can have completely different ideas—and vice versa.

    b. A manager must know how to give feedback objectively, not judgmentally.

        1. Being objective is very important when a manager is providing correction to workers on their performance or conduct.

        2. A manager who is judgmental sounds like he's attacking the person. The objective is to deal with what the individual *does*, not what he *is*.

    c. Feedback is an excellent way for a manager to show he's really listening.

    d. Even the most objective manager sometimes has to deal with *defensiveness*.

        1. Attacking the person who's being defensive only makes him more defensive.

        2. A person becomes defensive when he feels he's being attacked. When this happens, a manager should try to find out why the person feels that way.

        3. A manager sometimes needs to back off when someone is being defensive and try again another time.

        4. The best defense against defensiveness is to be open and honest, to communicate clearly, and to listen responsively. Most people will trust others who behave this way.

        5. A worker should understand that giving performance feedback is part of a manager's job and listening to it is part of a worker's job.

    e. A manager who expects to give feedback must learn to seek and accept it himself—in any form.

    f. Accepting feedback doesn't necessarily mean agreeing with what's said, but it does mean listening carefully and using the information.

5. *Being persuasive,* while an effective trait when combined with the other communication skills, isn't a substitute for them.

    a. Sometimes, though, a manager has to use persuasive skills—especially when there isn't time to develop open and trusting relationships, or when he has to make a decision quickly but needs others' support.

    b. The first requirement for being a persuasive manager is knowing the audience. This includes getting constant feedback in order to gauge the audience's reaction.

    c. The second requirement is being able to show the audience how what the manager wants them to do will help them meet their important goals.

    d. The best persuasion is often the selling that goes on inside the other person.

    e. Most of the time, what persuades (or doesn't persuade) others is the credibility of the persuader.

6. General Thoughts

    a. Communication is most effective when it's face-to-face and informal.

    b. This is particularly true of unpleasant situations, which should always be handled face-to-face, if possible. The manager shouldn't hide behind the impersonality of a written communication.

    c. Communicating in person is also a good rule for dealing with union representatives. The more informal and open these contacts are, the more useful they will be for both parties.

"Wow," said Helen. "That was quite a morning's work!"

BACK TO THE SKILLS MAXIMIZATION MODEL

The previous nine chapters have dealt with the basic activities of Phase One Management and its basic skill—communication. Together, these activities and the skill of communicating make up the Phase One Management block of our skills maximization model. This is what the model looks like now:

The next chapter will fill in one more block of the model—the fully successful workgroup.

StretchMeter 9: COMMUNICATING

1. I am open and honest with my workgroup.

NEVER   0   1   2   3   4   5   6   7   8   ALWAYS

2. I state things clearly.

NEVER   0   1   2   3   4   5   6   7   8   ALWAYS

3. I listen responsively to others.

NEVER   0   1   2   3   4   5   6   7   8   ALWAYS

4. I give and receive feedback.

NEVER   0   1   2   3   4   5   6   7   8   ALWAYS

5. I am persuasive.

NEVER   0   1   2   3   4   5   6   7   8   ALWAYS

6. I prefer to communicate face-to-face in difficult situations.

NEVER   0   1   2   3   4   5   6   7   8   ALWAYS

Communicating ASAP

1. Openness and honesty are often difficult, but they're the basis of successful communication. If you and your workgroup aren't used to interacting on that basis, start slowly. Here's one way to begin: Select a problem the group needs to work out (but not a major one). Perhaps it's something you've been trying to get them to do without telling them why, or a change that's coming that you haven't told them about yet. Whatever it is, call them together and tell them that you want to have more openness in the group. Then give them the information you've been holding back. If you can get reactions to it, so much the better. If you can't (and you probably can't at this stage), don't give up. Continue being open and asking for responses. After a while, the openness will become mutual.

2. Using clear and simple language isn't easy; most organizations encourage the reverse. The best place to start is with the two techniques mentioned in Chapter 11. First, say out loud what you want to write before you write it. Don't write it down until it *sounds* clear to you. Second, try out what you want to say (both written and spoken) on someone who's typical of your audience. Then ask him to paraphrase what you've said back to you. If he doesn't understand it, go back to the old drawing board.

3. Remember, effective listening means not only listening carefully but showing the other person that you're listening. Fortunately, it's an easy skill to practice—start today. At least five times a day for two weeks, listen responsively. Do it in a casual conversation at break or over lunch, when you're hearing a complaint, while getting directions from your boss—whenever. Spend at least 80 percent of that time listening. Use body language, short comments, and questions to show the person who's talking that you're listening. When the two weeks are over—do it for the rest of your life.

4. Communicating clearly, listening responsively, and using feedback can't be separated. If you're not comfortable using feedback, try ASAP 3—but concentrate on feedback. Questions can be part of it: "Do you mean that . . . ?" So can statements like "What it sounds to

me like you're saying is . . ." and "Let me make sure I understand you here. As you see it, . . ." When you're comfortable doing that, you can move on to feedback about behavior and performance. ("This is how what you did this morning struck me. . . .")

5. The best way to begin being persuasive is to understand your audience. They'll hear only what they *can* hear, so you need to think about what they can hear. Answer for yourself a few general questions: How old are they? How well-educated are they? How much do they know about the subject? You also need to answer specific questions, such as, "Has something happened to them to make them like (or dislike) what I'm proposing?" When you're comfortable doing this, move on to the next step (identifying what's important to them), and then the next, and the next.

6. It's hard to communicate face-to-face when things are tense—but that's when it's needed most. The way to get started is similar to that for ASAP 1: Pick one of your easier problems and talk to the person involved. *Don't* expect that he will respond positively (though he may). If things stay tense, they stay tense. Don't get emotionally involved; stay cool and stay with the problem. This type of communicating takes some getting used to, but it pays immense dividends.

CHAPTER 13

The Fully Successful Workgroup

SUCCESSFUL WORKGROUP	
Functioning as a Self-Managing Team	

In this chapter, you'll find useful information on:

The two characteristics of fully successful workgroups.

The reasons why this kind of workgroup is most successful.

What a manager can do to develop a fully successful workgroup.

Successful workers accomplish the group's function and leave the manager time for Phase Two Management. If successful workers make the quantum leap and become a fully successful workgroup, the group will accomplish its function even more effectively, and the manager will have even more time available for Phase Two Management.

WHAT IS A FULLY SUCCESSFUL WORKGROUP?

"Hey, Eleanor, got a minute?"

Eleanor looked up from her flow charts. Beverley Stallings, another senior programmer, was leaning against her cubicle. "What's up, Bev?"

"Mitzi and Angel have run into a snag with the mod they're working on. I thought maybe we could help them."

"Sure—I've got a headache from staring at these charts, anyway."

Eleanor and Beverley walked down the narrow aisle to Mitzi's cubicle, where she and Angel were frowning at a printout, tracing an invisible flow from page to page.

"Oh, hi," Mitzi said. "I know you're both busy, but if you could give us a hand, it sure would be great. Somehow or another, this thing gets lost in never-never land. Angel's been helping me for an hour, but, frankly, neither of us has any idea what's gone wrong."

Beverley and Eleanor bent over the printout. Everyone was quiet for a moment. "I'll bet that's it," Beverley said. She pointed at a line of code, then back up to a statement two pages earlier.

"Yep, I think you've got it. Mitzi, do you and Angel see what happened here?" For the next few minutes, Beverley and Eleanor explained the problem, until both Mitzi and Angel were nodding their heads vigorously.

"Listen, I have a thought," Eleanor said. "Lee is absolutely brilliant at loops. I have a couple of things I've been wanting to ask him, and I think he could show you several better ways to handle that particular step. Let's see if he's available."

"Not right now," Lee said as the four of them squeezed into his small office. "I promised Bernie I'd have this code ready for him when he comes back from lunch. He's drafting a talk I have to give tomorrow at the junior high, so I don't dare be late. Tell you what, though: Angel, if you and Mitzi will help me with this for half an hour, I'll meet the four of you for coffee in the conference room at three-thirty, and we can end up the day with our own symposium."

Clarence Wasserman, the section supervisor, watched the whole procedure from the door of his office. With him was Eduard Navarro, the Chief of Operations.

"Do you just let them run around like that?" Eduard asked. He looked disapproving.

"They're not running around—they're doing their jobs. You're watching a really successful workgroup in action."

"And just how do I tell they're so successful?"

"It's easy. They have the same two characteristics that any fully successful workgroup has." He paused.

Eduard waited a moment, then asked: "Are you going to tell me what they are?"

Clarence grinned. "First, they work together as a team. Second, they manage themselves. They just joined forces to solve a problem, and now they've organized their own training session. They don't know it yet, but I'm going to drop in on their little meeting and give them a new project to scope out for me."

"It sounds to me like you're letting them do your job."

"Nope. This afternoon, my job is to go to Supply and find out why we're almost out of three-part paper. C'mon, let's go have a cup of coffee and let them get their jobs done."

WHY IS A FULLY SUCCESSFUL WORKGROUP IMPORTANT?

Eduard and Clarence didn't talk any more that morning about successful workgroups. Clarence was a little disappointed. He felt good about the way his group operated and wanted to help Eduard see the advantages. On his way back to his office, he went over these advantages in his mind.

First, he said to himself, *self-management is the most effective form of management there is.* The people in his workgroup understood each other and knew how to make the most of each other's strengths. Once he'd made clear to them what needed to be done and when, he could leave most of the planning to them.

Just as important, because his group was a team, it was very stable and able to "roll with the punches." When something came up, they could deal with it themselves—they didn't have to wait for him to tell them what to do. When someone in the group was having problems, the others were there to help him.

For example, when Beverley was going through a messy divorce, she started drinking heavily, and it began to affect her work. Clarence psyched himself up to talk to her about it, and asked Eleanor for suggestions. "Don't fret it, boss," Eleanor had said. "We'll take care of this." The next afternoon, the whole group left together. Clarence had no idea what happened, but Beverley's drinking problem disappeared.

Clarence was also continually surprised at the quality of their ideas. Lee and Eleanor, who were the most creative of the group, seemed able to draw unexpected ideas from the others as well. Even Angel, who had been with the group less than six months, was coming up with valuable ideas.

One result of all this was his low turnover rate—which every manager in data processing envied. He knew that Bev, Eleanor and Lee had been contacted again and again about other jobs. The first time, Eleanor had said "yes" and had gone to work for an insurance company across town. Two weeks later she called and asked if she could have her old job back.

"Sure," Clarence had said, "but why? I can't pay you what they're paying."

"I never thought I'd say this to another human being, Clarence, but money just isn't that important. This place is dog-eat-dog. Yesterday, I tried to get one of the analysts to explain the claims system to me. He told me that was what manuals were for. That was the last straw. I want to come back!"

Yes, as far as Clarence was concerned, the benefits of a fully successful workgroup were evident. The final benefit was particularly important to him. Because he didn't have to spend his time managing their day-to-day work, he was free to build up his influence in the organization. He knew he'd get the three-part paper from Supply because he'd worked with the supply chief to smooth out the peaks and valleys in his section's requirements. And he was just about through with an analysis he was doing for his boss on programmers' workstations.

"Yep," he said to himself, "Eduard and the folks like him just don't know what they're missing."

HOW DO I DEVELOP A FULLY SUCCESSFUL WORKGROUP?

Clarence was roused from his reverie by Matt Chekhov, the newest manager in the Systems and Programs Division. "Clarence, do you have a moment? I need to ask you a few questions."

"Sure," Clarence said as Matt fell in step beside him. "What do I know that you want to know?"

"Everybody knows you've got one of the best sections in the organization—and people say it's because they work together. What makes a group of people a team?"

What Makes an Effective Team?

"Well," Clarence said, "there are many factors that make for an effective team, but I think these are the most important ones:

1. Members of the team have to share a common goal. All of my folks want to be good programmers. If one of them does sloppy work, the others are all over him. If one has a problem, the others jump in to help. They all believe that what they're doing is important, and they want to make sure they get it done and done well.[1]

2. They work together to accomplish almost everything. They know they're different from each other, and they recognize each other's special skills. Nobody can touch Lee when it comes to complex programming. On the other hand, no one turns out code as efficiently as Eleanor. They depend on each other's abilities, and because they do, almost nothing is a 'one-man job.' None of them gets any pleasure from being 'one-up' on the others.

---

[1]One way that's sometimes available to help the members of a workgroup develop a common goal is for them to compete with another workgroup—or several workgroups. This has to be done with care, however. If the group competes with another group where cooperation is necessary, the result can be harmful. If the competition gets so serious that one group attempts to sabotage or run down another, that can be harmful, too. But if you can encourage an honest competition, conducted with a certain amount of good humor, it can provide a useful common goal.

3. They make sure that all members support the group and its goals. Mitzi is attractive, and when she first joined the unit, she spent a lot of time enjoying the attention the men were giving her. It took some time, and the others upset her once or twice, but she got the word. She still likes to flirt, but now she confines it to breaks and after hours. On the job, she works as hard and as long as any of the others."

"I understand what you mean about teamwork," Matt said, "but what is this 'self-management' I've heard you mention?"

"It's exactly what it sounds like. All the things you usually think of as management—a workgroup functioning as a team can do them. Except for really big projects, my people plan their jobs for themselves; they work out who's going to do what. Oh, they come and check with me, but I almost never change anything. The few times when we've had vacancies, they've spent more time talking to the applicants than I have. They do most of the guiding and correcting, and they motivate themselves. They do permit me to delegate to them, and they're excellent at seeing to it that I support them. I must confess, though, that they do an awfully good job of supporting each other."[2]

Developing an Effective Team

"It sounds great," Matt said, "but just how do you go about developing a team?"

"Well," Clarence replied, "the first steps are pretty clear:

1. Successful workgroups require successful workers, so you take all of the Phase-One Management steps necessary to develop successful

---

[2]This book concentrates on developing successful workers and a successful workgroup. The manager needs to develop, too—as you may be beginning to notice. Clarence is a very mature manager. He encourages and enjoys the initiative and freedom his people have. If he weren't so secure himself, though, he might find the situation very threatening. Then he'd probably try to take back the initiative and freedom. This is not only difficult, it's demoralizing as hell for workers.

The moral? Your workgroup can't be more mature than you are. Make sure you develop along with them.

workers. You structure, select, guide, correct, motivate, delegate, and support.

2. Then, as individual workers develop, you begin to involve them with you in basic management tasks, such as guiding new workers. Correcting and supporting the new workers can tie right in with the guiding. As more workers develop, you involve them in planning, organizing, and setting priorities. As they get better and better, they'll begin to motivate and support one another. . . ."

"Excuse me for interrupting," Matt said, "but I need to ask you something here. You make it sound as if it's always good for a workgroup to work as a team. In the first programming job I had, the programmers all worked together, all right, but they spent most of their time figuring ways to beat the system. That was probably the least productive group I've ever worked with. I certainly wouldn't want my people to turn into that kind of group!"

"I don't blame you, either. You have to watch your timing and know your people. If they're not ready to take responsibility for effective performance as a team, one of three things will probably happen:

1. If they're not motivated to accomplish the assigned work, they may use teamwork as a 'license to steal.' They start working together to accomplish group goals that aren't the same as yours. They may limit the amount of work they'll do or set different priorities from yours, or just ignore any of your directions they don't like.

2. If they think you're trying to get them to do *your* work, they'll resent it. They'll probably force you to do all the managing, and they'll work as a team to see that you do.

3. They may be afraid of the idea of managing themselves. The responsibility and the risks may seem too great. If they don't trust you, they may even think you're setting them up to fail. Not only will they force you to manage, but this may set them back as a team.

"The result of any of these is that you'll be spending all your time on Phase One Management.

EXAMPLE: Premature Self-Management

"Okay, you guys, Marko wants us to work out a plan for converting to this new accounting system. What do you think we ought to do?"

"Whatever we do, let's be sure we take a long time doing it. If we play it right, we can make a full-time occupation out of this project until Christmas."

"Sounds good to me—and it serves him right, too. *He's* the manager. He's the one who's supposed to do the planning stuff. I've got plenty to do myself without doing his job, too."

"If you want my opinion, I think he wants to zap us. I haven't had any training in planning—have any of you guys? I didn't think so. He just wants us to fall flat on our faces so he won't have to promote any of us."

"Okay, here's what we'll do. Let's get something down on paper and go ask him about it. We'll take what he says, come back, and 'work on it some more.' Then we'll ask him for some help. That way, we'll get a real break from the day-to-day stuff, but he'll still have to do the work—and if anything goes wrong, he won't be able to blame it on us. How does that sound to you all? . . ."

(**WHAT IF** when they went to Marko the first time, he said, "No—I want you to do this by yourselves"? What might happen then?)

"Now that I've pointed out some of the problems, don't let them scare you. The key to building a successful team is knowing your people. You bring them along carefully. You let them take responsibility as they're ready for it. It's not that difficult; you just have to pay attention and be patient.

"Yes, I think I understand that. Now back to where we were before I interrupted. Beside developing your workers to be individually successful and encouraging them to take over self-management, what else do you do?"

Clarence smiled. "Here's where your influence with your boss and other managers comes in. The more control you and your workgroup have over your work, the more responsibility the workgroup will take for it. Let me give you an example: Let's say your boss wants to be sure that every job is done right, so she insists that you assign very specific duties to each worker. She also makes you personally inspect everything the group produces. Then she goes over it carefully herself—and often sends it back to you with directions to change it.

"How much self-management can your group have under these conditions? It's obvious—not much. So your people aren't going to be motivated to manage themselves—the payoff is too small.

"For them to become a team, you have to work on your second basic function as a manager: persuading your boss that you're a fully successful worker who can be left alone to do the job. If she gives you more freedom, you can give your workers more freedom."[3]

Developing Self-Management

Matt frowned ."I'm sure you don't mean that I just call a meeting one day and tell my group to take over. How do you go about giving them the responsibility for managing themselves?"

"Good question. You don't want to drop this on them all at once because it would probably scare them to death. The best thing to do is to find a small project or a problem that will be reasonably easy to solve. Get together with them and let them work on it. You may have to guide them, but don't *tell* them what to do.

"After they've had a little practice, give them a project or problem as a partial delegation. They work on it and give you recommendations, but you still make the final decision. When that's going well, move to a substantial delegation—where you let them make the decision, subject to your final approval. Then, full delegation. You do it the same way you would with an individual."

"It sounds good," Matt said, "but I'm not sure what kind of project or problem would be best as a starting point."

"Oh, there are plenty of them, if you know where to look. For instance, you could let your workgroup:

---

[3]See how everything a manager does is connected with everything else? The more successfully a manager does any function or activity, the easier it becomes to do the others.

1. Pick the new furniture for their work area and plan where to put it,
2. Work together to design a new report,
3. Decide what the vacation policy should be, and who gets preference when too many people want off at the same time, or
4. Solve a problem that one of them brings up to you.

"Those are the basics for developing self-management. Let me give you one other hint. Do you know what an 'informal leader' is?"

"I think you mean someone that the group respects and is willing to follow even though he doesn't have any formal authority."

"Right. Every group has an informal leader, sometimes several. When you're ready to start delegating to the team, you might try letting one of the informal leaders be the team leader. That way, you build on a structure that's already there."

EXAMPLE: Developing Self-Management

"Yesterday I asked the four of you to think about working out the new input procedures for the cost accounting system. What did you decide?"

"We talked about it, and we think we want to do it. We know how much the division needs it, and we think we understand it about as well as anyone. We're a little concerned, though—we thought *you* were supposed to do the planning for them."

"I can, if you want me to. Frankly, though, you've gotten so good that I'd like to turn you loose on something."

"We were hoping that was the case. But what happens if you 'turn us loose' and we fall flat on our faces?"

"Don't worry. I want you to work out a basic plan and then get back to me. If I think you're apt to get into trouble anywhere, we'll talk about it ahead of time. We'll also set up milestones and look at your progress each time you reach one of them. You've each done individual projects and done them well. This shouldn't be that different."

"We're still a little anxious, but we want to try it. The first thing we need to know about the procedures is . . ."

(WHAT IF the group had said they didn't really want to do it? How could the manager have taken back the responsibility for the project but still kept them involved?)

Some Final Tips

"Hey," Clarence said sudddenly, "I just noticed how late it is. I've got to be getting back to the office. But there are three more points I want to make:

> First of all, groups don't acquire skills magically; they have to learn them. If you have good workers in your group who are also good at communicating and working with others, they can train the others informally. If you don't, there's nothing wrong with sending your people to formal training sessions. And you might even want to sign up your informal leaders for some training on how to work with the group without dominating it. What's important is that your workers get the skills they need, not how it happens.
>
> Second, look out for workers who don't like working closely with others. There are lots of independent workers in the world, and they're often very good. If they think you're pressuring them to give up their independence, though, they may rebel, or even leave. You need to protect the independent workers and make sure they have the personal space they need. See that the others understand this, too. A good team appreciates the contribution each worker makes—even if the person isn't a tight member of the team.
>
> The last point is to pay attention to how you reward your workers. If you want a team, you need to reward your people for teamwork. When all of them, or a group of them, do a good job, reward the group—even if it's just writing them a note or hanging their picture on the wall. This doesn't mean you don't reward or recognize individuals; you do. In fact, if someone makes an individual contribution, be very careful not to blur it into a group effort. But keep on the lookout for successful team effort and never let it go unnoticed."

"Great!" Matt said. "I really appreciate your telling me this. I'll see you . . ."

"Not so fast. You and I both know how important feedback is, and you haven't given me any. I may be in a hurry, but I have plenty of time for you to give me . . ."

A QUICK SUMMARY

"Thanks for reminding me," Matt said and paused for a moment. "I think I remember most of what you said just now—and I remember some of what you've said before:

1. The first thing is something you didn't tell me today, but I've heard you say it a dozen times. Fully successful workgroups have two characteristics:

    a. They work together as a team.

    b. They manage themselves.

2. Then I've heard you give the reasons why this kind of workgroup is so successful:

    a. Self-management is the most effective form of management there is.

    b. Teams are stable, flexible, and able to 'roll with the punches.'

    c. Teams can produce very high quality ideas.

    d. Teams often have very low turnover rates.

    e. Teams give a manager time to spend on developing influence in the organization—Phase Two Management, I think someone called it.

3. Okay, that brings me up to today. If I remember right, this is what makes a successful team:

    a. They share a common goal.

    b. They accomplish projects together, as a team.

    c. They see that everybody in the group supports the team and its goals.

4. Let's see—then you told me that self-management means that the group does most of the basic management activities. They not only structure, guide, and correct themselves, but they even take part in selecting, motivating, and supporting each other. The manager still has to delegate and support the workgroup strongly, too.

5. After that, we talked about what has to be done to develop a fully successful workgroup:

    a. The manager lays the groundwork by structuring, selecting, guiding, correcting, motivating, delegating, and supporting effectively.

    b. As individual workers develop, the manager begins to involve them in his basic management tasks.

    c. The next requirement is this: if the workgroup is going to manage itself, it has to have control over most of what it does. If it doesn't, it's up to the manager to convince his boss to delegate this control.

    d. The manager should delegate self-management to the group gradually, starting with limited delegation on small projects or problems.

    e. Consider letting an informal leader be the team leader—at least to start.

6. You also told me about three situations in which trying to develop a self-managing group may fail:

    a. If the group isn't motivated to accomplish assigned work,

    b. If the group thinks the manager is trying to get them to do his work, or

    c. If they're afraid of the responsibility and risk involved in self-management.

    If I understood you right, the antidote for this is to know your people, bring them along carefully, and be patient.

7. That's when you got in a hurry and made three last points:

    a. Groups have to be trained in team skills, whether informally by the manager or group members, or through formal training.

    b. The manager must ensure that the group gives independent workers enough personal space.

    c. Finally—whew!—the manager needs to reward workers for working together."

MORE OF THE SKILLS MAXIMIZATION MODEL

The model is almost complete now. This chapter has added the last information on the workgroup. Here's how the model looks so far:

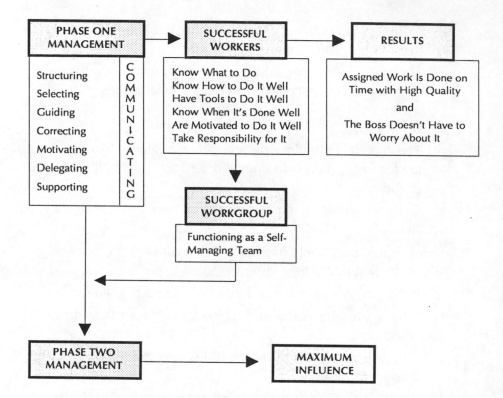

The next two chapters will complete the model by describing Phase Two Management in detail.

StretchMeter 10: SUCCESSFUL WORKGROUPS

1. My workgroup works together as an effective team.

NEVER   0   1   2   3   4   5   6   7   8   ALWAYS

2. My workgroup is self-managing.

NEVER   0   1   2   3   4   5   6   7   8   ALWAYS

3. The members of my workgroup share a common goal.

NEVER   0   1   2   3   4   5   6   7   8   ALWAYS

4. My workgroup and I have a great deal of control over the work.

NEVER   0   1   2   3   4   5   6   7   8   ALWAYS

5. I reward my workers for working together as a team.

NEVER   0   1   2   3   4   5   6   7   8   ALWAYS

6. I have time for Phase Two Management.

NEVER   0   1   2   3   4   5   6   7   8   ALWAYS

A Successful Workgroup ASAP

1. Up to this point, this book has dealt with the activities *you* need to do and the skills that *you* as a manager need to acquire. The ASAPs have been focused on the skills *you* needed to develop. In this chapter, the focus is on your *workgroup*. If they aren't ready to function as an effective team, there's nothing you can do to change the situation quickly. If they are ready, you should be applying the team-building ideas described in this chapter.

2. What was said in ASAP 1 about teamwork also goes for self-management. There's no single thing you can do to produce it—but if your team is ready for it, you should be following the steps in this chapter to help them accomplish it.

3. You can't force the members of your workgroup to share a common goal, but you can move them in that direction. This is your function as a leader—setting goals for the workgroup to which everyone can commit himself. If you haven't been doing that, *now* is the time to start. Within the next week, develop at least one goal for the group and present it to them. Keep bringing up the goal at strategic points for several months—until the group is sure you mean it and will stick to it. Then add another goal, and another, forming a coordinated group of goals. Don't forget the most important characteristic of successful goals, though: They must be goals that appeal to the workgroup, individually and collectively.[4]

4. Gaining control over your work and developing a successful workgroup go hand in hand. Each helps the other. Chapter 12 contained a number of steps to follow to persuade your boss that you—and your workgroup—are successful. Refer back to them and start working.

---

[4]Goals can be short-term or long-term. For instance, you might set a short-term goal of "cutting defectives by 20 percent" and a long-term goal of "keeping defectives under 1 percent." Or, you might have a short-term goal that your workgroup will "raise productivity by 10 percent" and a long-term goal that it will "consistently be one of the three most productive in the division." The group should be able to accomplish some goals in a few weeks or months—or even days—to give them a sense of their own success. Other goals should stretch them for years.

5. Rewarding your workers for producing results as a team is something you can begin right away. Much of what you need is in Chapter 8. Begin right now to make it clear that you want your people to work together—and that cooperation will be rewarded. Watch carefully for cooperation, and when you find it, reward it—even if it's just a verbal pat on the back. If the cooperation really helps accomplish something, reward it boldly. And keep rewarding it.

6. Having time for Phase Two Management is an outgrowth of successful Phase One Management. If you've done Phase One Management right, you now have the time for Phase Two. The next two chapters describe what Phase Two Management is and how to do it.

CHAPTER 14

Phase Two
Management, Part I

PHASE TWO MANAGEMENT	
Maximum Influence	
With Other Managers	
With Your Boss	

In this chapter, you'll find useful information on:

> The importance of influence.
>
> What influence really is.
>
> The key groups you need to influence (your suppliers, your customers, and your boss).
>
> The three steps required to develop influence.

These are the activities you can spend time on after you've developed successful workers and, hopefully, a successful workgroup.

WHAT IS EFFECTIVE PHASE TWO MANAGEMENT?

TO: Recognition Committee

SUBJECT: Nomination for "Up-and-Comer of the Year"

This department nominates Mr. Thomas Monahan as the organization's "Up-and-Comer of the Year."

Tom Monahan has been a manager under my supervision for just over three years. Six months after he moved into his position, his unit went from next-to-last place in our productivity measures to first place. In the two-and-a-half years since then, his unit has been in first place three times, second once, and third once. All one has to do is walk into his area to see how skillful Tom's workers are and how well they work together while still being individually productive. For the last five quarters, at least six of the ten top producers in this department have been in his unit.

However, Tom's contribution to the organization goes beyond increased productivity. Because he is so efficient at managing his people, he can devote a great deal of time to working with his peers and myself. In this, he has made himself invaluable to us. Here are some examples:

1. All of the data from Tom's unit is given to the department's data branch for input into the automated system. Before he took over, the error rate on the input was quite high, and there was constant friction between the two units. Each blamed each other for the errors. During Tom's service in the position, the error rate has fallen to less than 20 percent of what it was. He accomplished this by meeting with the manager of the data branch and working with her to identify the causes of the errors and eliminate them. Together, they worked out a set of procedures that are now being implemented department-wide.

2. One of the major products of Tom's unit is a workload planning document that is used throughout the department. This document was once very controversial, provoking constant complaints that it was

unrealistic and did not take account of enough
factors. One of Tom's first initiatives when he
took over the position was to meet with the other
four unit managers to discuss the document. This
first meeting evolved into a series of monthly
meetings, lasting almost a year, that resulted in
significant changes to the document. It is now used
with almost no complaint by the entire department.
The five managers have continued to meet on a
monthly basis and have made a number of further
improvements in the workflow between their units.

3. Perhaps Tom's greatest contribution, however, has
    been his ability to understand the "broader pic-
    ture" in the department. I have assigned him almost
    every project requiring department-wide coordina-
    tion for the last two years. He not only has good
    working relationships with the other units, but he
    has a surprising understanding of their work. His
    recommendations are accepted without dissent most
    of the time, which is all the more surprising be-
    cause they are often innovative. For instance, it
    was his research and recommendations that led to
    the department's highly successful customer aware-
    ness system.

4. Finally, nothing illustrates Tom's contribution
    more than his willingness to work as part of a
    team. At his initiative, I have begun to assign
    more significant projects to other managers in the
    department. He has volunteered to assist with these
    projects but has kept unobtrusively in the back-
    ground. Because of his team attitude, other manag-
    ers constantly seek his aid, and I do not believe
    there has been a single department-wide project
    over the past 18 months to which he has not made a
    significant contribution.

In short, I believe Tom Monahan is one of this
organization's truly up-and-coming managers and feel he
should be recognized as such.

                                    Gloria Maxwell
                                    Departmental Manager
                                    Information Systems

WHY IS EFFECTIVE PHASE TWO MANAGEMENT IMPORTANT?

"Well, Gloria, they tell me that you nominated Tom for 'Up-and-Comer of the Year.' The smart money says he'll get it."

"I certainly hope so. If ever anyone deserved it, he does."

"I know you think very highly of him—but I've never quite understood why. Several of your other managers' units are just as productive, and those managers don't wander around the organization as much as he does."

"That's just the point: his unit produces just as much as anyone else's, and he's more useful to the department as a whole than any of them. Let me give you two examples:

1. Tom has helped me develop the department into much more of a team. Those other managers, who stay in their work areas and don't 'wander around,' used to fight among themselves a great deal about who did what to whom and why. Tom has really helped reduce friction. It's not Paradise yet, but they're a lot more willing to work together than they used to be.

2. Tom is tremendously helpful to me personally. I used to fuss and fume about the things I wanted to get done but didn't have the time to do. I still don't have the time to do them—but he does. I think he's finished four special projects so far this year, and he's working on another two or three. I've sent a couple of them on to the Chairman, with nothing more than cosmetic changes. You can't imagine how my standing with the Front Office has improved because of his work."

"It sounds to me like he works 18 hours a day and has something on everyone else in your department."

"I know what you mean—but that's not how it is at all. Oh, Tom's a hard worker, all right, but so are most of my managers. It's what he accomplishes in the time he's at work that's significant. He doesn't have to do it all himself or force other people to do it because they have confidence in him; they trust him."

"It does sound like he has influence."

"That's the right word. Other managers *want* to work with him. In fact, so do I. In so many ways, he's the glue that really holds the operation together."

"It sounds great, Gloria, but it's gonna be quite a shock in the Front Office when they find out that a reformed alcoholic in his early fifties is their 'Up-and-Comer of the Year . . . .'"

HOW DO I BECOME AN EFFECTIVE PHASE TWO MANAGER?

Being "Political"

"Tom, we're friends, right?"

"Yes, I think so. Why?"

"I really want to ask you something, but I don't want you to get mad."

"Okay, I consider myself warned, Rosina. Shoot."

"The news is all over the place that you've been nominated as the organization's 'Up-and-Comer of the Year.' Because you're my friend, I'm really glad for you. But it bothers me to think that you got nominated because . . . because you're . . . I don't know any other way to say it— because you're so *political*!"

Tom laughed. "You really hate to say that, don't you?"

"Of course—doesn't everybody? I'd like to think that people get recognized because they do good work, not because they can pull strings."

"Rosina, I understand what bothers you, but I don't think I do that. Before I answer, though, tell me what you mean by 'political.'"

"That's not hard. Being 'political' is doing what politicians do: making deals, trading favors for favors, getting by on who you know instead of what you can do—the whole lousy schmear."

"Believe me, that isn't how I operate. Let me see if I can explain the difference to you. First of all, how well do you think I do as a manager with my own workgroup?"

"I guess you do okay."

"I do a lot better than okay. My people are one of the top two or three workgroups in the department. They produce a lot, they have high quality standards, and they work together. And if that weren't the case, I wouldn't want to be nominated for Up-and-Comer or anything like that. All right so far?"

"Yes—I'm really glad you said that."

"I understand that my first responsibility is to see that my workgroup produces and that my boss doesn't have to worry about us. I've done that by developing a successful workgroup. It's called Phase One Management. What you're talking about is Phase Two Management. It's just as important as Phase One, but you can't do it effectively until you've been successful at Phase One. . . ."

"Phase Two Management is politics?!" Rosina interrupted.

"Politics" and Influence

"No! Now please hear me out before you jump to conclusions. Phase Two Management is mostly building influence in the organization. Let me say right up front that this helps me personally. I wouldn't be nominated for anything if I didn't have influence. But that's not its basic purpose. I've developed influence so I can get my job done better by helping other managers and my boss get their jobs done better."

"That sounds fancy, but exactly what is 'influence'?"

"Influence is nothing more than the ability to get other people to do what you want them to—willingly. It's not the same thing as power. Having power means you can force people to do what you want. You get it because you're the boss or because you have the connections or the money or whatever. It doesn't make any difference what the other person wants—you get what you want."

"Is influence really different from power?"

"It sure is. Oh, I do some flat-out bargaining, and a number of people owe me favors I'll collect some day. But it's much more than that. The important thing about having influence is that people *want* to work with me. They believe that I'll be helpful to them and that I won't take advantage of them. They think they can get what they want best by teaming up with me."

EXAMPLE: Exercising Influence

"Tom, we're having a tremendous problem between Data Systems and Human Resources. They're virtually not speaking to each other—which means that our personnel and pay actions are running horrendously behind. A couple of us would like to get together and see what we might do to help things. We want you to join us. . . ."

"Tom, Maury told me that you've worked out a sharp training plan that will move some of your clerks up to your career positions. Would you be willing to show me what you did and help me set up the same kind of program for some of my people?"

"Tom, no matter what Edna and I try to do, the relationship between Purchasing and Accounting is completely bogged down in red tape. Do you think you could get together with us in the next week or so? We're hoping that you might see some ways to simplify things that we've been overlooking."

(**WHAT IF** these managers had been *told* to ask Tom for help? Would they have approached him in the same way?)

"Your idea of influence sounds okay."

"It is okay—and it's important. Each of us is dependent on our boss, our customers, out suppliers, and a few other key people in the organization. Let's run through these critical relationships:

First, there's your *boss*. If your boss doesn't have confidence in you, you won't get much freedom and responsibility. Your people will be in the same boat because you can't delegate to them what you don't have. If this lack of confidence is big enough, you'll never be able to develop a fully successful workgroup—which means your employees won't be all they can be. This isn't just some kind of noble idea. Workers who can't develop, lose out on promotions. It's just as important to them as to you that you have influence with your boss.

Next, there are your *customers*. What about the people who use what you produce? Your section does financial reports for the entire department. What happens if you don't have any influence with the people who use the reports? What happens if they think the reports aren't good, if they refuse to work with your people to resolve problems, if all they do is blame you? Your job gets much harder. If things are bad enough, your customers go to your boss—and you're back trying to build up influence with her again.

Then you have your *suppliers*. Every manager lives and dies by his suppliers. What happens when you can't get a large enough budget? When no one will expedite repairing your computer? When the forms you need aren't ready at the printer's? Again, it makes your job harder. It makes it harder to satisfy your customers, which makes it harder to satisfy your boss. See how they all pile up?

Finally, there are a few *others* who matter: your boss's boss, the internal auditors, the people in your headquarters staff office, probably a few more. They don't have the day-to-day impact on your job, but you still have to be concerned about them."

"Wow! I've never thought about it that way."

"Lots of managers don't—and it gets them into trouble. If my boss, my customers, and my suppliers aren't willing to work with me, life is going to be hard. The time I could have spent building up good relationships with them is going to be used up in 'fighting fires' and trying to justify things to people.

EXAMPLE: When You Don't Have Influence

"Gee, Walt, I'm sorry I can't help you. I know you need those new forms. We put in the order for them as quickly as we could, but you know how the system is—once your order is in it, there's nothing we can do. Again, I'm real sorry. . . ."

"Walt, we're getting tired of the mistakes your people are making. You keep asking me to help you figure out what's causing them—but that's *your* responsibility. My job is to tell you when you don't meet the division's standards. Well, I'm telling you! If you don't get your people shaped up, I'm going to the boss—and you can explain to her why you can't do your job. . . ."

"Walt, I don't like to interfere in our field operations, but I'm afraid I need to this time. Mr. Brezinski keeps calling me because the reports your section gives him are always late. You know how important service to the operating people is to me, so I think you'd better send me in a get-well plan this week. . . ."

(**WHAT IF** Walt had influence? How might each situation have been different?)

"On the other hand," Tom continued, "if I have good relationships— if I have influence—my job gets much easier. Now I can work with my boss, my customers, or my suppliers to resolve the problems we have together. Maybe that's the biggest difference right there: if I don't have influence, people will probably see me and my workgroup as part of the problem. If I have influence, they're more apt to see us as part of the solution.

"If I have influence, if people want to work with me so we can help each other be successful—that makes me successful and helps me advance my career. But I think it makes me successful for the right reasons. It makes me successful because I'm useful to the organization. Does this sound so bad?"

"Not when you put it that way. Maybe this thing you call 'Phase Two Management' *is* important. But how do you go about doing it? How do you get influence?"

Developing Influence

"I'm a lot more comfortable with this question than your first one. I could talk for an hour and only give you half an answer—but don't worry, I won't. I think there are three steps you have to take if you want to develop influence.

"First, I think you have to understand *what other people want from situations.* If I'm dealing with someone who knows and trusts me, and who's concerned about what I want, this is easy. We just tell each other what we want.

"A lot of the time, though, it isn't that simple—particularly if we haven't dealt with each other before. That means I have to ask smart questions and listen hard to the answers. I may have to listen to the other person's body language—notice things such as when they sit forward and look interested, and when they slouch back and begin to look a little bored.

"However I do it, my first step is to build up the clearest picture I can of what the other person's 'stake' is in the matter."

Rosina grinned. "This is certainly strange. We started off talking about how to get what you want, and here you are saying that the first thing is to find out what the other person wants."

"It is indeed. But then I go on to the second step: I try to set things up so that *we can both get what we need out of the situation.*"

"Oh, you mean find a compromise?"

"Not unless there's just no better way. Sometimes I do have to compromise, but when that happens neither of us feels good about it. I'm talking about working to find a solution that comes as close as possible to giving both of us what we need. When you compromise, nobody is really a winner. When you find a solution that meets everyone's real needs, *everybody* is a winner. Some people call this a 'win–win' situation, and I agree."

EXAMPLE: "Needs" versus "Wants"

Union negotiations had been going on for several days. In that time, management's representative had already negotiated several changes in the contract's language. He had begun arguing still another change when the union chief's negotiator interrupted him:

"Look, you may not have what you want, but you have what you *need.* Now, let's get on to something else."*

(**WHAT IF** the management negotiator had insisted on negotiating more changes on that subject? What would the union negotiator's reaction have been? What if the union negotiator hadn't had a good grasp of management's needs?)

*That exchange really happened. I know because I was the management negotiator. My union counterpart had a very clear sense of what management really needed from the contract, as opposed to what we merely wanted. He and I did, in fact, move on to the next article.

"I hadn't thought of it before, but it makes sense to try to see that everybody wins."

"Yes, Rosina, it does—and that takes us right into the third step: I may know what other people want, I may want to help them find a way to get it—but if I can't deliver for them, none of it matters. The third step is *being able to deliver the solution*. An effective manager, a manager who has influence, is one who can deliver for others.

"Look how important that is with your workgroup. If you can't deliver for them, they'll get discouraged. They'll start believing they can't count on you, so they won't.

"The same is true with other managers. You can learn what's really important to them and try to see that everybody wins. But if nothing comes of it, if you can't help them come up with a solution, you won't have been much use. And they'll try to find somebody who is."

"I can understand that easily enough. But it sounds terribly demanding."

"It is. In a minute I'll give you some tips on the best way to do it. For starters, though, you need to realize that I have some very good helpers— my workgroup. The first part of delivering is for us to do our job. When my group produces a product that meets our customers' needs, we're already building influence. We've already solved one problem for our customers—how to get a quality product. That's quite a lot.

"If I have a successful workgroup, though, they can help in another way. I can delegate some of my Phase Two Management to them. I do this carefully because it only works if my workgroup is *very* good. If they are, though, they can build influence—particularly with our suppliers and customers."

"Another new idea. I would never have thought of that. But certainly your workgroup can't do it all?"

"Oh, no. It's like any other kind of delegation: You don't delegate something until you have it under control and know they're ready for it. Then you do delegate it, so you have time to work the more difficult and important problems."

"Excuse me for interrupting you, Tom, but how do you tell the 'more difficult and important' problems?"

"Good question. You'll have to wait just a moment, though, while we go out this door and into the next chapter. . . ."

CHAPTER 15

Phase Two
Management, Part II

PHASE TWO MANAGEMENT
Maximum Influence
With Other Managers
With Your Boss
By Responsive, Synthesizing, Problem Solving

In this chapter, you'll find more useful information on:

The importance of unstructured problems.

The difference between technical, interpersonal, and synthesizing skills.

The most effective way to build influence in the organization is to be effective at solving—and helping others solve—unstructured problems.

THE HEART OF PHASE TWO MANAGEMENT

Identifying the "More Difficult and Important" Problems

Tom closed the door behind them. "That didn't take long. Now, you wanted to know how to tell the 'more difficult and important' problems: by the two characteristics that this kind of problem has.

"First of all, the more difficult and important problems stand out. When an organization has routine, run-of-the-mill problems, none of them is particularly obvious. Even those that are more 'serious' don't stand out that distinctly from the rest. An important problem is easy to recognize: People talk about it; perhaps they've tried to solve it once or twice and failed; they may even be preoccupied with it.

"Second, this type of problem is difficult to define. Some people call such problems 'unstructured.' A structured problem is one that's easy to state; everybody agrees on what it is and how to attack it. When you have an unstructured problem, though, people have very different opinions about what the 'real' problem is."

EXAMPLE: How to Recognize an Unstructured Problem

A young man got his MBA from a fine university and went to work for a large organization. After a year or so, his boss called him in and suggested that he look for employment elsewhere—it seemed he just wasn't working out.

As soon as he got over his disappointment, the young man did look for other jobs. While he was looking, he described his situation in a letter to a friend. Here is part of what he said:

> At the university, they gave me a good education in problem solving. If someone would just bring me a problem to solve, I know I could solve it. But around here, all they ever have are *messes!*

"Messes" is a word used in many organizations to describe unstructured problems. Here's another example. Your boss calls and says:

> "The organization is going to install a new payroll system in three months, and I want you to arrange training for the input clerks."

This is a structured problem. It's perfectly clear what you should do to solve it.

But suppose your boss says:

"The turnover in this branch is 35 percent a year, and I want you to do something about it."

Now what are you going to do? (Hint: if the answer seems easy, you don't understand unstructured problems yet.)

(**WHAT IF** your boss had said: "Our workers need more training"? Is that a structured or unstructured problem?)

"Thanks," Rosina said, "I think I understand now."

The Three Kinds of Skills

"You're welcome. Now, back to the 'more difficult and important' problems. I mentioned a little while ago that the significant thing about Phase Two Management is that it makes you useful to the organization. Well, working on this type of problem is where the payoff really comes.

"I want you to think of everything you and I do in terms of three overall kinds of skills: technical skills, interpersonal skills, and synthesizing skills. This is what they mean:

1. *Technical skills* are the skills you need to do a particular line of work. You have high technical skills if you're good at being a carpenter, attorney, supply clerk, or nurse. The better you become at these skills, the more easily you can use them to solve the difficult problems of the occupation.

2. *Interpersonal skills* are the skills you use when you deal with other people. Almost all workers have to have some of these skills, and some workers, such as salespeople and social workers, use them as primary job skills. Managers use interpersonal skills constantly because they can only get their jobs done by working with other people. That's why communication is such a critical skill for managers—you just can't work with other people unless you communicate well with them.

3. *Synthesizing skills* form the third group. Actually, it's difficult to know just what to call them. They're thinking skills—but a specific kind of thinking skills. They're the skills that allow you to take things that appear separate and see a unifying pattern to them. Every manager has to have them: You have to take the separate individuals and skills in your workgroup and pull them into a working team. But it's the people in the higher management jobs who really have to develop these skills. Upper-level managers must be able to pull together all the different kinds of activities that occur in an organization and make decisions that work best for the entire organization.

EXAMPLE: Technical, Interpersonal, and Synthesizing Skills

The distinctions Tom is making are important. Here are more examples that might help make the differences clearer:

1. Helping to work out a more sharply focused marketing plan,

    Helping Marketing and R&D set up a working group to coordinate their activities, or

    Helping to develop a company policy that establishes a systematic way for Marketing to make inputs to R&D decisions, and vice versa.

2. Meeting with your engineering workgroup to simplify the design of your new product,

    Meeting with a team from Manufacturing to try and reduce the hostility between your two departments, or

    Meeting with a team from R&D, Manufacturing, and Marketing to identify potential new markets for the next two years.

3. Showing the chief of the motor pool how to set up trip records quickly and easily,

    Sitting in on a meeting between the chief of the motor pool and his drivers to help them bring to the surface and discuss the morale problem in the branch, or

    Working with the chief of the motor pool and the organization's training officer to develop a training program that will prepare drivers to move into inspector positions—to reduce the turnover among drivers and get candidates for hard-to-fill inspector positions.

You've probably noticed by now that technical skills are used in the first part of each sequence, interpersonal skills in the second, and synthesizing skills in the third.

Did you also notice that as you move from technical through interpersonal to synthesizing, the problems become less structured? Synthesizing skills are a necessity if you want to deal effectively with unstructured problems.

(**WHAT IF** you try to deal with a problem that requires synthesizing skills by using technical skills? What do you think might happen?)

"Does all that make sense to you, Rosina?"

"Yes, it does."

"Let's take a look at where we are. We've decided that we're going to find out what the real needs of other managers are; we're going to try to find solutions that meet both their needs and ours; and we're going to deliver a solid result for them. We're going to do this by concentrating on the more difficult and important problems. Now the question is: How are we going to do this?"

"I have a feeling that you're about to tell me the answer."

Using Technical Skills

"Well, we could start by concentrating on technical problems. You're an accountant. You could communicate to the managers you work with that you'd like to help them with any of their accounting problems—you know, setting up their budgets, controlling their expenses, that sort of thing. Now, what do you suppose those managers will say about you once you deliver effectively by helping them solve their accounting problems?"

"Well, they'll say I'm a good accountant. . . . That's okay, I guess, but I don't think that most managers have that many accounting problems."

"They don't. If you concentrate on solving technical problems, you're going to have a problem yourself—in fact, two problems:

1. Most problems that managers run up against don't fall into someone else's specialty. At a time when an organization is going to a new budget system, you can be very helpful. But day in and day out, most

managers don't need help solving a lot of accounting problems—or supply problems or personnel problems or what have you.

2. How much good does it do you and your workgroup for you to be known as a really good accountant? Accounting is what your people do. If you become the expert, you limit what they can do, how far they can go. And you get yourself typecast as a technician, not a manager.

"In other words, it's not a very good strategy. There's nothing wrong with solving accounting problems for other managers occasionally—it keeps you in touch with what's important to them in your field. On the whole, though, you're better off developing your workers to handle these problems. Then you can make them available to other managers, support them, and let them be the super technicians."

Using Interpersonal Skills

"I see what you mean. Since I'm a manager, I need to be working with interpersonal problems."

"The answer is a 'yes, but . . . ,' so let's look at it. You're not going to solve accounting problems. Instead, you're going to solve problems by working with other people and helping them work together. You're going to be the kind of person that other people want on committees and workgroups. You're going to be the kind of person other managers come to for advice on people problems. How does that sound to you?"

"It sounds much better. Everybody may not have accounting problems, but *everybody* has people problems. Besides, working well with other people is what managers are supposed to do. This way gives me plenty of problems to try and help with, and it shows people that I'm an effective manager."

"Right. But there's a problem here, too. You want people to believe you're a good manager. And having good interpersonal skills is going to help you tremendously with other managers. In fact, your boss may depend on you for them. . . ."

"Then what's the problem?" Rosina blurted out.

"It's simple. People see you as a very good first-level manager—but they don't necessarily see you as someone who's ready for promotion to the next level. I want to talk about that in a minute, but let me say something more about delegating here.

"Everyone expects your people to be good at their technical skills. But what about their interpersonal skills? Which is going to make them more promotable: being good workers or being good at handling people?"

"Oh, being good at handling people. That's what being a manager is about. Aha—now I'm following you. You're going to tell me to delegate some of my interpersonal problems to my workers. That way, they can develop their interpersonal skills and be more competitive for promotion."

"Right—but your workers aren't the only ones who profit from it. Just think what a workgroup you'd have if all of your people had super interpersonal skills. It's back to the point I was making earlier. If the organization is being run properly, the skills and activities that make you promotable are the ones that will pay off for the organization. If you delegate some interpersonal problem solving to your workers, you'll gain as much from it as they will."

"That makes excellent sense."

EXAMPLE: Delegating That Requires Interpersonal Skills

This is how Tom delegated to his workers duties that required good interpersonal skills:

> When Tom took over his job, relations were really tense between his unit and the data unit, which input his unit's transactions (remember the award nomination?). He made that friction a priority and spent time working with Helen Sizdek, the data unit manager, to improve the situation.
>
> It took time, but the two of them came up with very workable solutions—enough so that their ideas are being used department-wide.
>
> Tom and Helen resolved the most serious problems, but that didn't mean there were no problems left or that new problems wouldn't come along. Because most of these problems would be routine, however, solving them wasn't a good use of Helen and Tom's time. Instead, they formed a small problem-solving committee.
>
> The committee has two workers from each unit, and the membership rotates every quarter. The committee meets once a month to see if

there are matters that require its attention. Usually, these problems can be resolved in one or two meetings. Only once has this not been true; in that case, Tom and Helen met with the committee and helped work out a solution.

In a few pages, you'll see how significant such a delegation can be for both you and your workers.

(**WHAT IF** Tom and Helen had kept meeting to solve the routine problems? Why wouldn't that have been a good use of their time?)

Using Synthesizing Skills

"Now I'll bet you're about to get to synthesizing skills."

"Right. If you really want to be useful to the organization and make the right kind of name for yourself, you'll concentrate on problems that require synthesizing skills. Not only are good synthesizing skills extremely important, they're extremely rare."

"I understand why they might be rare, but why are they so important?"

"The higher you go in the organization, the more diverse the areas are you have to handle. Rosina, you have to understand two kinds of work in your unit: accounting and budgeting. Your boss has to fit those two together with data processing, purchasing, and auditing. His boss has to tie those five areas together with . . ."

"I get your point."

"Good—then you can see how important it is to your boss for you to be good at understanding and drawing together different functions. That way he can let you work on some of his problems that require synthesizing skills. There's nothing I do that's more valuable to my boss than being able to take this kind of broad view.

"It's almost as valuable for the other managers you work with. If you understand the 'big picture,' you can work with them to make decisions that will be approved by your boss. It increases your ability to deliver results for them.

"I might add that this is where working with other managers is extremely useful. The more you work with them, the better you're going to understand their functions—and the easier it'll be to see the overall picture. And the more you see the big picture, the better you can understand what you and other managers do and how it all fits together."

"That sounds almost like 'motherhood and apple pie.'"

"Believe me, it isn't. It's hard work. Remember, when you're working at this level, the problems aren't very well structured. You spend a tremendous amount of time just figuring out what the problem is before you can work at solving it."

"Whew," Rosina said. "When I said something to you about 'politics,' I had no idea that this is where it would lead. Not only do I feel better about what I thought was your 'political' side, but you've given me some very helpful information. You go on; I'm going to stop here and make some quick notes on what you said."

"Good idea. I'm glad you thought it was useful."

Rosina slipped into a vacant cubicle and pulled out her pad. This is what she wrote:

A QUICK SUMMARY

1. As a manager, I'm dependent on my boss, my customers, my suppliers, and a few other key people in the organization.

2. Because I need their cooperation and help, I need to develop influence with all of them.

3. To develop influence, I need to

    a. Understand what my boss, my customers, my suppliers, and the others need from situations,

    b. See that we both get what we need out of a situation (create a "win–win" solution), and

    c. Be able to deliver the solution.

4. To develop maximum influence, I need to be good at dealing with the "more difficult and important" problems which

    a. Stand out, and

    b. Are "unstructured" problems (problems that people have trouble even defining).

5. There are three kinds of skills I can use in trying to identify and solve problems:

    a. *Technical skills*—those needed to do a particular line of work.

    b. *Interpersonal skills*—those needed to deal with other people.

   c. *Synthesizing skills*—those needed to pull together different functions for the good of the organization.

6. I should delegate the solving of most technical problems to my
workgroup and give them opportunities to work on interpersonal
problems, too. I should concentrate on the problems that require
synthesizing skills.

7. When I'm good at Phase Two Management, my workgroups, other
managers, and my boss all benefit. Being successful at Phase One
and Phase Two Management is also what will best enhance my
career.

THE SKILLS MAXIMIZATION MODEL—COMPLETE!

The last block is now in place. The complete model shown preceding
page 1 of this book has now been developed. As a last reminder, here it
is again.

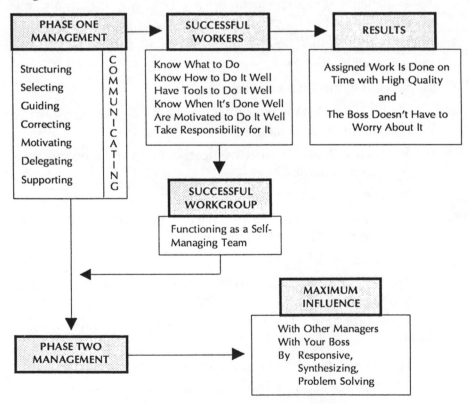

StretchMeter 11: PHASE TWO MANAGEMENT

1. My workgroup operates as a team and is self-managing.

NEVER   0   1   2   3   4   5   6   7   8   ALWAYS

2. I understand what the key people I deal with need.

NEVER   0   1   2   3   4   5   6   7   8   ALWAYS

3. I work to produce "win–win" solutions with others.

NEVER   0   1   2   3   4   5   6   7   8   ALWAYS

4. I deliver the solutions others need.

NEVER   0   1   2   3   4   5   6   7   8   ALWAYS

5. I enjoy working with unstructured problems.

NEVER   0   1   2   3   4   5   6   7   8   ALWAYS

6. I use good synthesizing skills.

NEVER   0   1   2   3   4   5   6   7   8   ALWAYS

7. I delegate problems requiring technical skills to my workgroup.

NEVER   0   1   2   3   4   5   6   7   8   ALWAYS

8. I delegate problems requiring interpersonal skills to my workgroup.

NEVER   0   1   2   3   4   5   6   7   8   ALWAYS

Phase Two Management ASAP

1. Item 1 on the StretchMeter is a trick question. If your workgroup doesn't operate as a team and isn't self-managing, you'll have less time available for Phase Two Management. Spend some time on Phase Two Management, but make sure you're still working to develop a fully successful workgroup.

2. If you don't understand what the key people you deal with need, you can't exercise effective influence. Select someone you deal with regularly (a supplier or customer will be best). Devote the next two weeks to finding out what's important to him. Ask, observe, listen. Make a list of what you believe his most important objectives are. Then do the same with the other managers who are key to you.

3. Using "win–win" strategies begins with knowing what others want. Make sure you do. If possible, start with a relatively easy problem that can be worked out with a manager who is already on good terms with you. Say up front that you want to find a "win–win" solution. Work with him to find it and don't quit until you do. Gradually expand this approach to more and more managers and more and more difficult problems.

4. If others don't believe you will deliver, you don't really have influence. Use the same approach as in ASAP 3, but this time concentrate on finding a solution you can *deliver*. Don't work on any other problems until you deliver the solution.

5. If you don't enjoy working with unstructured problems, it may be simply lack of practice. It may also be the desire to have problems that come in nice, safe packages. Neither will do. Unfortunately, there's no quick way to develop a feel for unstructured problems. One good strategy is to find a mentor.[1] You can also understand this kind of problem better by reading books, such as those by Tom Peters

---

[1]In case you're not familiar with the term, a "mentor" in this context is a more senior manager who's willing to take you under his wing and help your development. Having a mentor who is concerned about you is an excellent way to develop Phase Two skills in general, and to develop the ability to understand unstructured problems in particular.

and Robert Waterman that are mentioned in the Suggested Readings at the end of this book.

6. If you don't have good synthesizing skills, it's probably because you're not adept yet at dealing with unstructured problems. A mentor is very helpful here. You can also learn by finding an exemplar—a senior manager who has these skills—and observing how he deals with unstructured problems.

7. If your workgroup is successful, you should be delegating most problems requiring technical skills to your workers—so you'll have time for Phase Two Management. If you're not delegating the technical problems to them, they're not yet successful. If you think you've developed successful workers and you're still holding on to the challenging technical problems, STOP! Right now! Beginning tomorrow morning, delegate every new technical problem to them. (There, that one was simple, wasn't it?)

8. Here again, if your workgroup is successful, you should be delegating to them at least some problems requiring interpersonal skills. If you're not, start now. Identify your worker or group of workers with the best interpersonal skills. Select an interpersonal problem involving another unit. Get the person (people) and the problem together. Delegate it as completely as you're comfortable with. Keep on in the same direction, following the guidance for successful delegation in Chapter 9.

Epilogue

"**W**ell, Louise, I haven't seen you for awhile. I thought maybe you'd lived up to your threat and quit." Tim brushed the crumbs from the table in front of him and sat down.

"You won't believe what she's been telling us, Tim. She's not the same woman you were talking to a couple of months ago." Jennie was sitting beside Louise and grinning.

"Yeah, I heard what she's been saying, but I don't know that I believe any of it." That came from Barry, who was sitting across from Jennie.

"All this sounds *very* interesting. Louise, would you bring me up to date?"

"Sure, Tim. It's nothing that special, really. You remember how frustrated I was a number of weeks ago when we were talking about what it was like to be a first-level manager?"

Tim nodded.

"Well, I read this book I found at the bookstore on surviving as a new manager. I started doing some of the things it suggested, and I'll be darned if they didn't work."

"What kinds of things?" Tim was clearly interested.

"Well, I don't want to go into it right now, but it has to do with developing successful workers and then using your influence to help the organization solve problems. I can tell you the name of the book if you'd like.

Barry started to say something, but Louise kept on. "Anyway, things started improving. Then personnel scheduled me into their basic supervisory course, which cleared up a lot of the things I'd read about in the book.

"The course gave me some other ideas, too, and I've been trying them as well. As a matter of fact, the reason I'm here now is that the ideas worked so well, my group kicked me out." She paused, a slight grin on her lips.

"Kicked you out?" Barry said.

"Whatta you mean, they worked so well?" This was from Jennie.

"I don't see what you mean at all," Tim said, looking as puzzled as he sounded.

"It's really quite simple. We have that new Archer project to do, and my people told me to get out of their hair until they get it organized. So I did."

She paused a moment. "You know, sometimes management is a blast! But I've got to go now. I promised the boss I'd write up a new procedure on tardiness, and I need to finish it this afternoon. Anybody want to work on it with me?"

Nobody did. They were all too busy.

Suggested Readings:
Your Own
Management University

Y ou have access to your own management university where you can
learn anything you want to know about management. This university, which has great teachers who are always available and whose
services are free, is called the public library. (If you have access to a
university library, so much the better.) Even a small town library has the
ability to track down any book you want through interlibrary loan. And
most libraries now have audio and video tapes that cover aspects of management.

Here is a list of some of the books you might want to seek out in your
management university:

One of the first you might read is *Analyzing Performance Problems:
or, You Really Oughta Wanna*, by John Mager and Peter Pipe
(Belmont, Calif.: Pittman Management and Training Division of
Pittman Learning, 1984). This very short, very readable book has no
equal as a basic resource for identifying *why* the right performance
isn't happening.

Another is *Haga's Law* by William James Haga and Nicholas
Acocella (New York: Morrow, 1980). This book is about bureaucra-
cies and how they get to be that way. If you work for an organization
that has 100 people or more, it probably was, is, or soon will be a
bureaucracy. Haga's Law will help you understand why bureaucracy happens and how not to encourage it. In addition, it's hilarious.
But, then, what would you expect from a book with the subtitle "Why
Nothing Works and No One Can Fix It and the More We Try the
Worse It Gets"?

Wait until you've been a manager at least six months, then read
Managing Management Time, by William Oncken (Englewood
Cliffs, N.J.: Prentice-Hall, 1984). In my judgment, this is the classic
work on delegation. It's also a very down-to-earth book on managing. If you find some things in Oncken's book that remind you of this
one, it's because I've been heavily influenced by his work.

Another, more traditional book on controlling your time is *Time
Power*, by Charles R. Hobbs (New York: Harper & Row, 1987),
which provides a strong introduction to the topic of time management. It also contains some good management philosophy.

If you want to do some serious management reading, read Paul Hersey and Ken Blanchard's *Management of Organizational Behavior*, 5th edition (Englewood Cliffs, N.J.: Prentice-Hall, 1982). I first read this in the 1970s, and it still influences me.

There are three other writers who've influenced me greatly in the last decade:

It's heavy going, but *Human Competence*, by Thomas F. Gilbert (New York: McGraw-Hill, 1978) is a real eye-opener about human potential. It also had a great impact on the shape of this book.

Let's face it, I'm a Peters and Waterman junkie. I'm referring, of course, to Tom Peters and Robert Waterman, co-authors of *In Search of Excellence* (New York: Harper & Row, 1982)—one of the most popular management books ever written. Peters has written two subsequent books, *A Passion for Excellence*, with Nancy Austin (New York: Random House, 1985) and *Thriving on Chaos: Handbook for a Management Revolution* (New York: Alfred A. Knopf, 1987). Waterman's second book is *The Revival Factor: How the Best Get and Keep the Competitive Edge* (New York: Bantam, 1987). This is major-league, broad-gauge management writing that's still easy to read.

I have difficulty relating to situations where individuals are troubled because they work for or with female managers. Perhaps it's because my primary background is in personnel management, which has been open to women for years; perhaps it's because I've worked for and with excellent female managers. You may not have had this experience. If you're troubled by being a woman manager, or working for or with a woman manager, you might want to read:

Women in Charge: Dilemmas of Women in Authority, by Aileen Jacobson (New York: Van Nostrand Reinhold, 1985).

Dealing with problem employees is never easy. There are numerous books on the subject. One you might start with is:

Problem Employees: How to Improve Their Performance, by Peter Wylie and Mardy Grothe (Belmont, Calif.: Pittman Management and Training Division of Pittman Learning, 1981).

There are hundreds of management books, many of them good, many of them not so good, which aren't on this list. And that brings me to my final point:

The way to learn about management is (1) to manage, and (2) to read as much as possible about management. All books (including, alas, this one) try to sell one approach. The way you gain a balanced viewpoint is to read a variety of books, with different philosophies. If you read just one book a month, after five years, you will have read *60* books—and that's a real management education!

Index